C-1071   CAREER EXAMINATION SERIES

*This is your
PASSBOOK for...*

Accounting Assistant

*Test Preparation Study Guide
Questions & Answers*

COPYRIGHT NOTICE

This book is SOLELY intended for, is sold ONLY to, and its use is RESTRICTED to individual, bona fide applicants or candidates who qualify by virtue of having seriously filed applications for appropriate license, certificate, professional and/or promotional advancement, higher school matriculation, scholarship, or other legitimate requirements of education and/or governmental authorities.

This book is NOT intended for use, class instruction, tutoring, training, duplication, copying, reprinting, excerption, or adaptation, etc., by:

1) Other publishers
2) Proprietors and/or Instructors of "Coaching" and/or Preparatory Courses
3) Personnel and/or Training Divisions of commercial, industrial, and governmental organizations
4) Schools, colleges, or universities and/or their departments and staffs, including teachers and other personnel
5) Testing Agencies or Bureaus
6) Study groups which seek by the purchase of a single volume to copy and/or duplicate and/or adapt this material for use by the group as a whole without having purchased individual volumes for each of the members of the group
7) Et al.

Such persons would be in violation of appropriate Federal and State statutes.

PROVISION OF LICENSING AGREEMENTS – Recognized educational, commercial, industrial, and governmental institutions and organizations, and others legitimately engaged in educational pursuits, including training, testing, and measurement activities, may address request for a licensing agreement to the copyright owners, who will determine whether, and under what conditions, including fees and charges, the materials in this book may be used them. In other words, a licensing facility exists for the legitimate use of the material in this book on other than an individual basis. However, it is asseverated and affirmed here that the material in this book CANNOT be used without the receipt of the express permission of such a licensing agreement from the Publishers. Inquiries re licensing should be addressed to the company, attention rights and permissions department.

All rights reserved, including the right of reproduction in whole or in part, in any form or by any means, electronic or mechanical, including photocopying, recording, or by any information storage and retrieval system, without permission in writing from the Publisher.

Copyright © 2024 by
National Learning Corporation

212 Michael Drive, Syosset, NY 11791
(516) 921-8888 • www.passbooks.com
E-mail: info@passbooks.com

PUBLISHED IN THE UNITED STATES OF AMERICA

PASSBOOK® SERIES

THE *PASSBOOK® SERIES* has been created to prepare applicants and candidates for the ultimate academic battlefield – the examination room.

At some time in our lives, each and every one of us may be required to take an examination – for validation, matriculation, admission, qualification, registration, certification, or licensure.

Based on the assumption that every applicant or candidate has met the basic formal educational standards, has taken the required number of courses, and read the necessary texts, the *PASSBOOK® SERIES* furnishes the one special preparation which may assure passing with confidence, instead of failing with insecurity. Examination questions – together with answers – are furnished as the basic vehicle for study so that the mysteries of the examination and its compounding difficulties may be eliminated or diminished by a sure method.

This book is meant to help you pass your examination provided that you qualify and are serious in your objective.

The entire field is reviewed through the huge store of content information which is succinctly presented through a provocative and challenging approach – the question-and-answer method.

A climate of success is established by furnishing the correct answers at the end of each test.

You soon learn to recognize types of questions, forms of questions, and patterns of questioning. You may even begin to anticipate expected outcomes.

You perceive that many questions are repeated or adapted so that you can gain acute insights, which may enable you to score many sure points.

You learn how to confront new questions, or types of questions, and to attack them confidently and work out the correct answers.

You note objectives and emphases, and recognize pitfalls and dangers, so that you may make positive educational adjustments.

Moreover, you are kept fully informed in relation to new concepts, methods, practices, and directions in the field.

You discover that you are actually taking the examination all the time: you are preparing for the examination by "taking" an examination, not by reading extraneous and/or supererogatory textbooks.

In short, this PASSBOOK®, used directedly, should be an important factor in helping you to pass your test.

ACCOUNTING ASSISTANT

DUTIES
Performs subprofessional accounting work involving the compilation and maintenance of financial records and accounts in accordance with established procedures and regulations. Performs related duties as required.

SCOPE OF THE EXAMINATION
The written test will cover knowledge, skills and/or abilities in such areas as:
1. Fundamentals of account keeping and bookkeeping;
2. Clerical operations with letters and numbers;
3. Arithmetic computation and reasoning;
4. Understanding and interpreting tabular material; and
5. Understanding and interpreting written material.

HOW TO TAKE A TEST

I. YOU MUST PASS AN EXAMINATION

A. *WHAT EVERY CANDIDATE SHOULD KNOW*

Examination applicants often ask us for help in preparing for the written test. What can I study in advance? What kinds of questions will be asked? How will the test be given? How will the papers be graded?

As an applicant for a civil service examination, you may be wondering about some of these things. Our purpose here is to suggest effective methods of advance study and to describe civil service examinations.

Your chances for success on this examination can be increased if you know how to prepare. Those "pre-examination jitters" can be reduced if you know what to expect. You can even experience an adventure in good citizenship if you know why civil service exams are given.

B. *WHY ARE CIVIL SERVICE EXAMINATIONS GIVEN?*

Civil service examinations are important to you in two ways. As a citizen, you want public jobs filled by employees who know how to do their work. As a job seeker, you want a fair chance to compete for that job on an equal footing with other candidates. The best-known means of accomplishing this two-fold goal is the competitive examination.

Exams are widely publicized throughout the nation. They may be administered for jobs in federal, state, city, municipal, town or village governments or agencies.

Any citizen may apply, with some limitations, such as the age or residence of applicants. Your experience and education may be reviewed to see whether you meet the requirements for the particular examination. When these requirements exist, they are reasonable and applied consistently to all applicants. Thus, a competitive examination may cause you some uneasiness now, but it is your privilege and safeguard.

C. *HOW ARE CIVIL SERVICE EXAMS DEVELOPED?*

Examinations are carefully written by trained technicians who are specialists in the field known as "psychological measurement," in consultation with recognized authorities in the field of work that the test will cover. These experts recommend the subject matter areas or skills to be tested; only those knowledges or skills important to your success on the job are included. The most reliable books and source materials available are used as references. Together, the experts and technicians judge the difficulty level of the questions.

Test technicians know how to phrase questions so that the problem is clearly stated. Their ethics do not permit "trick" or "catch" questions. Questions may have been tried out on sample groups, or subjected to statistical analysis, to determine their usefulness.

Written tests are often used in combination with performance tests, ratings of training and experience, and oral interviews. All of these measures combine to form the best-known means of finding the right person for the right job.

II. HOW TO PASS THE WRITTEN TEST

A. NATURE OF THE EXAMINATION

To prepare intelligently for civil service examinations, you should know how they differ from school examinations you have taken. In school you were assigned certain definite pages to read or subjects to cover. The examination questions were quite detailed and usually emphasized memory. Civil service exams, on the other hand, try to discover your present ability to perform the duties of a position, plus your potentiality to learn these duties. In other words, a civil service exam attempts to predict how successful you will be. Questions cover such a broad area that they cannot be as minute and detailed as school exam questions.

In the public service similar kinds of work, or positions, are grouped together in one "class." This process is known as *position-classification*. All the positions in a class are paid according to the salary range for that class. One class title covers all of these positions, and they are all tested by the same examination.

B. FOUR BASIC STEPS

1) Study the announcement

How, then, can you know what subjects to study? Our best answer is: "Learn as much as possible about the class of positions for which you've applied." The exam will test the knowledge, skills and abilities needed to do the work.

Your most valuable source of information about the position you want is the official exam announcement. This announcement lists the training and experience qualifications. Check these standards and apply only if you come reasonably close to meeting them.

The brief description of the position in the examination announcement offers some clues to the subjects which will be tested. Think about the job itself. Review the duties in your mind. Can you perform them, or are there some in which you are rusty? Fill in the blank spots in your preparation.

Many jurisdictions preview the written test in the exam announcement by including a section called "Knowledge and Abilities Required," "Scope of the Examination," or some similar heading. Here you will find out specifically what fields will be tested.

2) Review your own background

Once you learn in general what the position is all about, and what you need to know to do the work, ask yourself which subjects you already know fairly well and which need improvement. You may wonder whether to concentrate on improving your strong areas or on building some background in your fields of weakness. When the announcement has specified "some knowledge" or "considerable knowledge," or has used adjectives like "beginning principles of..." or "advanced ... methods," you can get a clue as to the number and difficulty of questions to be asked in any given field. More questions, and hence broader coverage, would be included for those subjects which are more important in the work. Now weigh your strengths and weaknesses against the job requirements and prepare accordingly.

3) Determine the level of the position

Another way to tell how intensively you should prepare is to understand the level of the job for which you are applying. Is it the entering level? In other words, is this the position in which beginners in a field of work are hired? Or is it an intermediate or advanced level? Sometimes this is indicated by such words as "Junior" or "Senior" in the class title. Other jurisdictions use Roman numerals to designate the level – Clerk I, Clerk II, for example. The word "Supervisor" sometimes appears in the title. If the level is not indicated by the title, check the description of duties. Will you be working under very close supervision, or will you have responsibility for independent decisions in this work?

4) Choose appropriate study materials

Now that you know the subjects to be examined and the relative amount of each subject to be covered, you can choose suitable study materials. For beginning level jobs, or even advanced ones, if you have a pronounced weakness in some aspect of your training, read a modern, standard textbook in that field. Be sure it is up to date and has general coverage. Such books are normally available at your library, and the librarian will be glad to help you locate one. For entry-level positions, questions of appropriate difficulty are chosen – neither highly advanced questions, nor those too simple. Such questions require careful thought but not advanced training.

If the position for which you are applying is technical or advanced, you will read more advanced, specialized material. If you are already familiar with the basic principles of your field, elementary textbooks would waste your time. Concentrate on advanced textbooks and technical periodicals. Think through the concepts and review difficult problems in your field.

These are all general sources. You can get more ideas on your own initiative, following these leads. For example, training manuals and publications of the government agency which employs workers in your field can be useful, particularly for technical and professional positions. A letter or visit to the government department involved may result in more specific study suggestions, and certainly will provide you with a more definite idea of the exact nature of the position you are seeking.

III. KINDS OF TESTS

Tests are used for purposes other than measuring knowledge and ability to perform specified duties. For some positions, it is equally important to test ability to make adjustments to new situations or to profit from training. In others, basic mental abilities not dependent on information are essential. Questions which test these things may not appear as pertinent to the duties of the position as those which test for knowledge and information. Yet they are often highly important parts of a fair examination. For very general questions, it is almost impossible to help you direct your study efforts. What we can do is to point out some of the more common of these general abilities needed in public service positions and describe some typical questions.

1) General information

Broad, general information has been found useful for predicting job success in some kinds of work. This is tested in a variety of ways, from vocabulary lists to questions about current events. Basic background in some field of work, such as sociology or economics, may be sampled in a group of questions. Often these are principles which have become familiar to most persons through exposure rather than through formal training. It is difficult to advise you how to study for these questions; being alert to the world around you is our best suggestion.

2) Verbal ability

An example of an ability needed in many positions is verbal or language ability. Verbal ability is, in brief, the ability to use and understand words. Vocabulary and grammar tests are typical measures of this ability. Reading comprehension or paragraph interpretation questions are common in many kinds of civil service tests. You are given a paragraph of written material and asked to find its central meaning.

3) Numerical ability

Number skills can be tested by the familiar arithmetic problem, by checking paired lists of numbers to see which are alike and which are different, or by interpreting charts and graphs. In the latter test, a graph may be printed in the test booklet which you are asked to use as the basis for answering questions.

4) Observation

A popular test for law-enforcement positions is the observation test. A picture is shown to you for several minutes, then taken away. Questions about the picture test your ability to observe both details and larger elements.

5) Following directions

In many positions in the public service, the employee must be able to carry out written instructions dependably and accurately. You may be given a chart with several columns, each column listing a variety of information. The questions require you to carry out directions involving the information given in the chart.

6) Skills and aptitudes

Performance tests effectively measure some manual skills and aptitudes. When the skill is one in which you are trained, such as typing or shorthand, you can practice. These tests are often very much like those given in business school or high school courses. For many of the other skills and aptitudes, however, no short-time preparation can be made. Skills and abilities natural to you or that you have developed throughout your lifetime are being tested.

Many of the general questions just described provide all the data needed to answer the questions and ask you to use your reasoning ability to find the answers. Your best preparation for these tests, as well as for tests of facts and ideas, is to be at your physical and mental best. You, no doubt, have your own methods of getting into an exam-taking mood and keeping "in shape." The next section lists some ideas on this subject.

IV. KINDS OF QUESTIONS

Only rarely is the "essay" question, which you answer in narrative form, used in civil service tests. Civil service tests are usually of the short-answer type. Full instructions for answering these questions will be given to you at the examination. But in case this is your first experience with short-answer questions and separate answer sheets, here is what you need to know:

1) Multiple-choice Questions

Most popular of the short-answer questions is the "multiple choice" or "best answer" question. It can be used, for example, to test for factual knowledge, ability to solve problems or judgment in meeting situations found at work.

A multiple-choice question is normally one of three types—

- It can begin with an incomplete statement followed by several possible endings. You are to find the one ending which *best* completes the statement, although some of the others may not be entirely wrong.
- It can also be a complete statement in the form of a question which is answered by choosing one of the statements listed.

- It can be in the form of a problem – again you select the best answer.

Here is an example of a multiple-choice question with a discussion which should give you some clues as to the method for choosing the right answer:

When an employee has a complaint about his assignment, the action which will *best* help him overcome his difficulty is to
- A. discuss his difficulty with his coworkers
- B. take the problem to the head of the organization
- C. take the problem to the person who gave him the assignment
- D. say nothing to anyone about his complaint

In answering this question, you should study each of the choices to find which is best. Consider choice "A" – Certainly an employee may discuss his complaint with fellow employees, but no change or improvement can result, and the complaint remains unresolved. Choice "B" is a poor choice since the head of the organization probably does not know what assignment you have been given, and taking your problem to him is known as "going over the head" of the supervisor. The supervisor, or person who made the assignment, is the person who can clarify it or correct any injustice. Choice "C" is, therefore, correct. To say nothing, as in choice "D," is unwise. Supervisors have and interest in knowing the problems employees are facing, and the employee is seeking a solution to his problem.

2) True/False Questions

The "true/false" or "right/wrong" form of question is sometimes used. Here a complete statement is given. Your job is to decide whether the statement is right or wrong.

SAMPLE: A roaming cell-phone call to a nearby city costs less than a non-roaming call to a distant city.

This statement is wrong, or false, since roaming calls are more expensive.

This is not a complete list of all possible question forms, although most of the others are variations of these common types. You will always get complete directions for answering questions. Be sure you understand *how* to mark your answers – ask questions until you do.

V. RECORDING YOUR ANSWERS

Computer terminals are used more and more today for many different kinds of exams.

For an examination with very few applicants, you may be told to record your answers in the test booklet itself. Separate answer sheets are much more common. If this separate answer sheet is to be scored by machine – and this is often the case – it is highly important that you mark your answers correctly in order to get credit.

An electronic scoring machine is often used in civil service offices because of the speed with which papers can be scored. Machine-scored answer sheets must be marked with a pencil, which will be given to you. This pencil has a high graphite content which responds to the electronic scoring machine. As a matter of fact, stray dots may register as answers, so do not let your pencil rest on the answer sheet while you are pondering the correct answer. Also, if your pencil lead breaks or is otherwise defective, ask for another.

Since the answer sheet will be dropped in a slot in the scoring machine, be careful not to bend the corners or get the paper crumpled.

The answer sheet normally has five vertical columns of numbers, with 30 numbers to a column. These numbers correspond to the question numbers in your test booklet. After each number, going across the page are four or five pairs of dotted lines. These short dotted lines have small letters or numbers above them. The first two pairs may also have a "T" or "F" above the letters. This indicates that the first two pairs only are to be used if the questions are of the true-false type. If the questions are multiple choice, disregard the "T" and "F" and pay attention only to the small letters or numbers.

Answer your questions in the manner of the sample that follows:

32. The largest city in the United States is
    A. Washington, D.C.
    B. New York City
    C. Chicago
    D. Detroit
    E. San Francisco

1) Choose the answer you think is best. (New York City is the largest, so "B" is correct.)
2) Find the row of dotted lines numbered the same as the question you are answering. (Find row number 32)
3) Find the pair of dotted lines corresponding to the answer. (Find the pair of lines under the mark "B.")
4) Make a solid black mark between the dotted lines.

VI. BEFORE THE TEST

Common sense will help you find procedures to follow to get ready for an examination. Too many of us, however, overlook these sensible measures. Indeed, nervousness and fatigue have been found to be the most serious reasons why applicants fail to do their best on civil service tests. Here is a list of reminders:

- Begin your preparation early – Don't wait until the last minute to go scurrying around for books and materials or to find out what the position is all about.
- Prepare continuously – An hour a night for a week is better than an all-night cram session. This has been definitely established. What is more, a night a week for a month will return better dividends than crowding your study into a shorter period of time.
- Locate the place of the exam – You have been sent a notice telling you when and where to report for the examination. If the location is in a different town or otherwise unfamiliar to you, it would be well to inquire the best route and learn something about the building.
- Relax the night before the test – Allow your mind to rest. Do not study at all that night. Plan some mild recreation or diversion; then go to bed early and get a good night's sleep.
- Get up early enough to make a leisurely trip to the place for the test – This way unforeseen events, traffic snarls, unfamiliar buildings, etc. will not upset you.
- Dress comfortably – A written test is not a fashion show. You will be known by number and not by name, so wear something comfortable.

- Leave excess paraphernalia at home – Shopping bags and odd bundles will get in your way. You need bring only the items mentioned in the official notice you received; usually everything you need is provided. Do not bring reference books to the exam. They will only confuse those last minutes and be taken away from you when in the test room.
- Arrive somewhat ahead of time – If because of transportation schedules you must get there very early, bring a newspaper or magazine to take your mind off yourself while waiting.
- Locate the examination room – When you have found the proper room, you will be directed to the seat or part of the room where you will sit. Sometimes you are given a sheet of instructions to read while you are waiting. Do not fill out any forms until you are told to do so; just read them and be prepared.
- Relax and prepare to listen to the instructions
- If you have any physical problem that may keep you from doing your best, be sure to tell the test administrator. If you are sick or in poor health, you really cannot do your best on the exam. You can come back and take the test some other time.

VII. AT THE TEST

The day of the test is here and you have the test booklet in your hand. The temptation to get going is very strong. Caution! There is more to success than knowing the right answers. You must know how to identify your papers and understand variations in the type of short-answer question used in this particular examination. Follow these suggestions for maximum results from your efforts:

1) Cooperate with the monitor

The test administrator has a duty to create a situation in which you can be as much at ease as possible. He will give instructions, tell you when to begin, check to see that you are marking your answer sheet correctly, and so on. He is not there to guard you, although he will see that your competitors do not take unfair advantage. He wants to help you do your best.

2) Listen to all instructions

Don't jump the gun! Wait until you understand all directions. In most civil service tests you get more time than you need to answer the questions. So don't be in a hurry. Read each word of instructions until you clearly understand the meaning. Study the examples, listen to all announcements and follow directions. Ask questions if you do not understand what to do.

3) Identify your papers

Civil service exams are usually identified by number only. You will be assigned a number; you must not put your name on your test papers. Be sure to copy your number correctly. Since more than one exam may be given, copy your exact examination title.

4) Plan your time

Unless you are told that a test is a "speed" or "rate of work" test, speed itself is usually not important. Time enough to answer all the questions will be provided, but this does not mean that you have all day. An overall time limit has been set. Divide the total time (in minutes) by the number of questions to determine the approximate time you have for each question.

5) Do not linger over difficult questions

If you come across a difficult question, mark it with a paper clip (useful to have along) and come back to it when you have been through the booklet. One caution if you do this – be sure to skip a number on your answer sheet as well. Check often to be sure that you have not lost your place and that you are marking in the row numbered the same as the question you are answering.

6) Read the questions

Be sure you know what the question asks! Many capable people are unsuccessful because they failed to *read* the questions correctly.

7) Answer all questions

Unless you have been instructed that a penalty will be deducted for incorrect answers, it is better to guess than to omit a question.

8) Speed tests

It is often better NOT to guess on speed tests. It has been found that on timed tests people are tempted to spend the last few seconds before time is called in marking answers at random – without even reading them – in the hope of picking up a few extra points. To discourage this practice, the instructions may warn you that your score will be "corrected" for guessing. That is, a penalty will be applied. The incorrect answers will be deducted from the correct ones, or some other penalty formula will be used.

9) Review your answers

If you finish before time is called, go back to the questions you guessed or omitted to give them further thought. Review other answers if you have time.

10) Return your test materials

If you are ready to leave before others have finished or time is called, take ALL your materials to the monitor and leave quietly. Never take any test material with you. The monitor can discover whose papers are not complete, and taking a test booklet may be grounds for disqualification.

VIII. EXAMINATION TECHNIQUES

1) Read the general instructions carefully. These are usually printed on the first page of the exam booklet. As a rule, these instructions refer to the timing of the examination; the fact that you should not start work until the signal and must stop work at a signal, etc. If there are any *special* instructions, such as a choice of questions to be answered, make sure that you note this instruction carefully.

2) When you are ready to start work on the examination, that is as soon as the signal has been given, read the instructions to each question booklet, underline any key words or phrases, such as *least*, *best*, *outline*, *describe* and the like. In this way you will tend to answer as requested rather than discover on reviewing your paper that you *listed without describing*, that you selected the *worst* choice rather than the *best* choice, etc.

3) If the examination is of the objective or multiple-choice type – that is, each question will also give a series of possible answers: A, B, C or D, and you are called upon to select the best answer and write the letter next to that answer on your answer paper – it is advisable to start answering each question in turn. There may be anywhere from 50 to 100 such questions in the three or four hours allotted and you can see how much time would be taken if you read through all the questions before beginning to answer any. Furthermore, if you come across a question or group of questions which you know would be difficult to answer, it would undoubtedly affect your handling of all the other questions.

4) If the examination is of the essay type and contains but a few questions, it is a moot point as to whether you should read all the questions before starting to answer any one. Of course, if you are given a choice – say five out of seven and the like – then it is essential to read all the questions so you can eliminate the two that are most difficult. If, however, you are asked to answer all the questions, there may be danger in trying to answer the easiest one first because you may find that you will spend too much time on it. The best technique is to answer the first question, then proceed to the second, etc.

5) Time your answers. Before the exam begins, write down the time it started, then add the time allowed for the examination and write down the time it must be completed, then divide the time available somewhat as follows:
    - If 3-1/2 hours are allowed, that would be 210 minutes. If you have 80 objective-type questions, that would be an average of 2-1/2 minutes per question. Allow yourself no more than 2 minutes per question, or a total of 160 minutes, which will permit about 50 minutes to review.
    - If for the time allotment of 210 minutes there are 7 essay questions to answer, that would average about 30 minutes a question. Give yourself only 25 minutes per question so that you have about 35 minutes to review.

6) The most important instruction is to *read each question* and make sure you know what is wanted. The second most important instruction is to *time yourself properly* so that you answer every question. The third most important instruction is to *answer every question*. Guess if you have to but include something for each question. Remember that you will receive no credit for a blank and will probably receive some credit if you write something in answer to an essay question. If you guess a letter – say "B" for a multiple-choice question – you may have guessed right. If you leave a blank as an answer to a multiple-choice question, the examiners may respect your feelings but it will not add a point to your score. Some exams may penalize you for wrong answers, so in such cases *only*, you may not want to guess unless you have some basis for your answer.

7) Suggestions
    a. Objective-type questions
        1. Examine the question booklet for proper sequence of pages and questions
        2. Read all instructions carefully
        3. Skip any question which seems too difficult; return to it after all other questions have been answered
        4. Apportion your time properly; do not spend too much time on any single question or group of questions

5. Note and underline key words – *all, most, fewest, least, best, worst, same, opposite*, etc.
6. Pay particular attention to negatives
7. Note unusual option, e.g., unduly long, short, complex, different or similar in content to the body of the question
8. Observe the use of "hedging" words – *probably, may, most likely*, etc.
9. Make sure that your answer is put next to the same number as the question
10. Do not second-guess unless you have good reason to believe the second answer is definitely more correct
11. Cross out original answer if you decide another answer is more accurate; do not erase until you are ready to hand your paper in
12. Answer all questions; guess unless instructed otherwise
13. Leave time for review

b. Essay questions
1. Read each question carefully
2. Determine exactly what is wanted. Underline key words or phrases.
3. Decide on outline or paragraph answer
4. Include many different points and elements unless asked to develop any one or two points or elements
5. Show impartiality by giving pros and cons unless directed to select one side only
6. Make and write down any assumptions you find necessary to answer the questions
7. Watch your English, grammar, punctuation and choice of words
8. Time your answers; don't crowd material

8) Answering the essay question

Most essay questions can be answered by framing the specific response around several key words or ideas. Here are a few such key words or ideas:

M's: manpower, materials, methods, money, management
P's: purpose, program, policy, plan, procedure, practice, problems, pitfalls, personnel, public relations

a. Six basic steps in handling problems:
1. Preliminary plan and background development
2. Collect information, data and facts
3. Analyze and interpret information, data and facts
4. Analyze and develop solutions as well as make recommendations
5. Prepare report and sell recommendations
6. Install recommendations and follow up effectiveness

b. Pitfalls to avoid
1. *Taking things for granted* – A statement of the situation does not necessarily imply that each of the elements is necessarily true; for example, a complaint may be invalid and biased so that all that can be taken for granted is that a complaint has been registered

2. *Considering only one side of a situation* – Wherever possible, indicate several alternatives and then point out the reasons you selected the best one
3. *Failing to indicate follow up* – Whenever your answer indicates action on your part, make certain that you will take proper follow-up action to see how successful your recommendations, procedures or actions turn out to be
4. *Taking too long in answering any single question* – Remember to time your answers properly

IX. AFTER THE TEST

Scoring procedures differ in detail among civil service jurisdictions although the general principles are the same. Whether the papers are hand-scored or graded by machine we have described, they are nearly always graded by number. That is, the person who marks the paper knows only the number – never the name – of the applicant. Not until all the papers have been graded will they be matched with names. If other tests, such as training and experience or oral interview ratings have been given, scores will be combined. Different parts of the examination usually have different weights. For example, the written test might count 60 percent of the final grade, and a rating of training and experience 40 percent. In many jurisdictions, veterans will have a certain number of points added to their grades.

After the final grade has been determined, the names are placed in grade order and an eligible list is established. There are various methods for resolving ties between those who get the same final grade – probably the most common is to place first the name of the person whose application was received first. Job offers are made from the eligible list in the order the names appear on it. You will be notified of your grade and your rank as soon as all these computations have been made. This will be done as rapidly as possible.

People who are found to meet the requirements in the announcement are called "eligibles." Their names are put on a list of eligible candidates. An eligible's chances of getting a job depend on how high he stands on this list and how fast agencies are filling jobs from the list.

When a job is to be filled from a list of eligibles, the agency asks for the names of people on the list of eligibles for that job. When the civil service commission receives this request, it sends to the agency the names of the three people highest on this list. Or, if the job to be filled has specialized requirements, the office sends the agency the names of the top three persons who meet these requirements from the general list.

The appointing officer makes a choice from among the three people whose names were sent to him. If the selected person accepts the appointment, the names of the others are put back on the list to be considered for future openings.

That is the rule in hiring from all kinds of eligible lists, whether they are for typist, carpenter, chemist, or something else. For every vacancy, the appointing officer has his choice of any one of the top three eligibles on the list. This explains why the person whose name is on top of the list sometimes does not get an appointment when some of the persons lower on the list do. If the appointing officer chooses the second or third eligible, the No. 1 eligible does not get a job at once, but stays on the list until he is appointed or the list is terminated.

X. HOW TO PASS THE INTERVIEW TEST

The examination for which you applied requires an oral interview test. You have already taken the written test and you are now being called for the interview test – the final part of the formal examination.

You may think that it is not possible to prepare for an interview test and that there are no procedures to follow during an interview. Our purpose is to point out some things you can do in advance that will help you and some good rules to follow and pitfalls to avoid while you are being interviewed.

What is an interview supposed to test?

The written examination is designed to test the technical knowledge and competence of the candidate; the oral is designed to evaluate intangible qualities, not readily measured otherwise, and to establish a list showing the relative fitness of each candidate – as measured against his competitors – for the position sought. Scoring is not on the basis of "right" and "wrong," but on a sliding scale of values ranging from "not passable" to "outstanding." As a matter of fact, it is possible to achieve a relatively low score without a single "incorrect" answer because of evident weakness in the qualities being measured.

Occasionally, an examination may consist entirely of an oral test – either an individual or a group oral. In such cases, information is sought concerning the technical knowledges and abilities of the candidate, since there has been no written examination for this purpose. More commonly, however, an oral test is used to supplement a written examination.

Who conducts interviews?

The composition of oral boards varies among different jurisdictions. In nearly all, a representative of the personnel department serves as chairman. One of the members of the board may be a representative of the department in which the candidate would work. In some cases, "outside experts" are used, and, frequently, a businessman or some other representative of the general public is asked to serve. Labor and management or other special groups may be represented. The aim is to secure the services of experts in the appropriate field.

However the board is composed, it is a good idea (and not at all improper or unethical) to ascertain in advance of the interview who the members are and what groups they represent. When you are introduced to them, you will have some idea of their backgrounds and interests, and at least you will not stutter and stammer over their names.

What should be done before the interview?

While knowledge about the board members is useful and takes some of the surprise element out of the interview, there is other preparation which is more substantive. It *is* possible to prepare for an oral interview – in several ways:

1) Keep a copy of your application and review it carefully before the interview

This may be the only document before the oral board, and the starting point of the interview. Know what education and experience you have listed there, and the sequence and dates of all of it. Sometimes the board will ask you to review the highlights of your experience for them; you should not have to hem and haw doing it.

2) Study the class specification and the examination announcement

Usually, the oral board has one or both of these to guide them. The qualities, characteristics or knowledges required by the position sought are stated in these documents. They offer valuable clues as to the nature of the oral interview. For example, if the job involves supervisory responsibilities, the announcement will usually indicate that knowledge of modern supervisory methods and the qualifications of the candidate as a supervisor will be tested. If so, you can expect such questions, frequently in the form of a hypothetical situation which you are expected to solve. NEVER go into an oral without knowledge of the duties and responsibilities of the job you seek.

3) Think through each qualification required

Try to visualize the kind of questions you would ask if you were a board member. How well could you answer them? Try especially to appraise your own knowledge and background in each area, *measured against the job sought*, and identify any areas in which you are weak. Be critical and realistic – do not flatter yourself.

4) Do some general reading in areas in which you feel you may be weak

For example, if the job involves supervision and your past experience has NOT, some general reading in supervisory methods and practices, particularly in the field of human relations, might be useful. Do NOT study agency procedures or detailed manuals. The oral board will be testing your understanding and capacity, not your memory.

5) Get a good night's sleep and watch your general health and mental attitude

You will want a clear head at the interview. Take care of a cold or any other minor ailment, and of course, no hangovers.

What should be done on the day of the interview?

Now comes the day of the interview itself. Give yourself plenty of time to get there. Plan to arrive somewhat ahead of the scheduled time, particularly if your appointment is in the fore part of the day. If a previous candidate fails to appear, the board might be ready for you a bit early. By early afternoon an oral board is almost invariably behind schedule if there are many candidates, and you may have to wait. Take along a book or magazine to read, or your application to review, but leave any extraneous material in the waiting room when you go in for your interview. In any event, relax and compose yourself.

The matter of dress is important. The board is forming impressions about you – from your experience, your manners, your attitude, and your appearance. Give your personal appearance careful attention. Dress your best, but not your flashiest. Choose conservative, appropriate clothing, and be sure it is immaculate. This is a business interview, and your appearance should indicate that you regard it as such. Besides, being well groomed and properly dressed will help boost your confidence.

Sooner or later, someone will call your name and escort you into the interview room. *This is it.* From here on you are on your own. It is too late for any more preparation. But remember, you asked for this opportunity to prove your fitness, and you are here because your request was granted.

What happens when you go in?

The usual sequence of events will be as follows: The clerk (who is often the board stenographer) will introduce you to the chairman of the oral board, who will introduce you to the other members of the board. Acknowledge the introductions before you sit down. Do not be surprised if you find a microphone facing you or a stenotypist sitting by. Oral interviews are usually recorded in the event of an appeal or other review.

Usually the chairman of the board will open the interview by reviewing the highlights of your education and work experience from your application – primarily for the benefit of the other members of the board, as well as to get the material into the record. Do not interrupt or comment unless there is an error or significant misinterpretation; if that is the case, do not hesitate. But do not quibble about insignificant matters. Also, he will usually ask you some question about your education, experience or your present job – partly to get you to start talking and to establish the interviewing "rapport." He may start the actual questioning, or turn it over to one of the other members. Frequently, each member undertakes the questioning on a particular area, one in which he is perhaps most competent, so you can expect each member to participate in the examination. Because time is limited, you may also expect some rather abrupt switches in the direction the questioning takes, so do not be upset by it. Normally, a board member will not pursue a single line of questioning unless he discovers a particular strength or weakness.

After each member has participated, the chairman will usually ask whether any member has any further questions, then will ask you if you have anything you wish to add. Unless you are expecting this question, it may floor you. Worse, it may start you off on an extended, extemporaneous speech. The board is not usually seeking more information. The question is principally to offer you a last opportunity to present further qualifications or to indicate that you have nothing to add. So, if you feel that a significant qualification or characteristic has been overlooked, it is proper to point it out in a sentence or so. Do not compliment the board on the thoroughness of their examination – they have been sketchy, and you know it. If you wish, merely say, "No thank you, I have nothing further to add." This is a point where you can "talk yourself out" of a good impression or fail to present an important bit of information. Remember, *you close the interview yourself.*

The chairman will then say, "That is all, Mr. _____, thank you." Do not be startled; the interview is over, and quicker than you think. Thank him, gather your belongings and take your leave. Save your sigh of relief for the other side of the door.

How to put your best foot forward

Throughout this entire process, you may feel that the board individually and collectively is trying to pierce your defenses, seek out your hidden weaknesses and embarrass and confuse you. Actually, this is not true. They are obliged to make an appraisal of your qualifications for the job you are seeking, and they want to see you in your best light. Remember, they must interview all candidates and a non-cooperative candidate may become a failure in spite of their best efforts to bring out his qualifications. Here are 15 suggestions that will help you:

1) Be natural – Keep your attitude confident, not cocky

If you are not confident that you can do the job, do not expect the board to be. Do not apologize for your weaknesses, try to bring out your strong points. The board is interested in a positive, not negative, presentation. Cockiness will antagonize any board member and make him wonder if you are covering up a weakness by a false show of strength.

2) Get comfortable, but don't lounge or sprawl

Sit erectly but not stiffly. A careless posture may lead the board to conclude that you are careless in other things, or at least that you are not impressed by the importance of the occasion. Either conclusion is natural, even if incorrect. Do not fuss with your clothing, a pencil or an ashtray. Your hands may occasionally be useful to emphasize a point; do not let them become a point of distraction.

3) Do not wisecrack or make small talk

This is a serious situation, and your attitude should show that you consider it as such. Further, the time of the board is limited – they do not want to waste it, and neither should you.

4) Do not exaggerate your experience or abilities

In the first place, from information in the application or other interviews and sources, the board may know more about you than you think. Secondly, you probably will not get away with it. An experienced board is rather adept at spotting such a situation, so do not take the chance.

5) If you know a board member, do not make a point of it, yet do not hide it

Certainly you are not fooling him, and probably not the other members of the board. Do not try to take advantage of your acquaintanceship – it will probably do you little good.

6) Do not dominate the interview

Let the board do that. They will give you the clues – do not assume that you have to do all the talking. Realize that the board has a number of questions to ask you, and do not try to take up all the interview time by showing off your extensive knowledge of the answer to the first one.

7) Be attentive

You only have 20 minutes or so, and you should keep your attention at its sharpest throughout. When a member is addressing a problem or question to you, give him your undivided attention. Address your reply principally to him, but do not exclude the other board members.

8) Do not interrupt

A board member may be stating a problem for you to analyze. He will ask you a question when the time comes. Let him state the problem, and wait for the question.

9) Make sure you understand the question

Do not try to answer until you are sure what the question is. If it is not clear, restate it in your own words or ask the board member to clarify it for you. However, do not haggle about minor elements.

10) Reply promptly but not hastily

A common entry on oral board rating sheets is "candidate responded readily," or "candidate hesitated in replies." Respond as promptly and quickly as you can, but do not jump to a hasty, ill-considered answer.

11) Do not be peremptory in your answers

A brief answer is proper – but do not fire your answer back. That is a losing game from your point of view. The board member can probably ask questions much faster than you can answer them.

12) Do not try to create the answer you think the board member wants

He is interested in what kind of mind you have and how it works – not in playing games. Furthermore, he can usually spot this practice and will actually grade you down on it.

13) Do not switch sides in your reply merely to agree with a board member

Frequently, a member will take a contrary position merely to draw you out and to see if you are willing and able to defend your point of view. Do not start a debate, yet do not surrender a good position. If a position is worth taking, it is worth defending.

14) Do not be afraid to admit an error in judgment if you are shown to be wrong

The board knows that you are forced to reply without any opportunity for careful consideration. Your answer may be demonstrably wrong. If so, admit it and get on with the interview.

15) Do not dwell at length on your present job

The opening question may relate to your present assignment. Answer the question but do not go into an extended discussion. You are being examined for a *new* job, not your present one. As a matter of fact, try to phrase ALL your answers in terms of the job for which you are being examined.

Basis of Rating

Probably you will forget most of these "do's" and "don'ts" when you walk into the oral interview room. Even remembering them all will not ensure you a passing grade. Perhaps you did not have the qualifications in the first place. But remembering them will help you to put your best foot forward, without treading on the toes of the board members.

Rumor and popular opinion to the contrary notwithstanding, an oral board wants you to make the best appearance possible. They know you are under pressure – but they also want to see how you respond to it as a guide to what your reaction would be under the pressures of the job you seek. They will be influenced by the degree of poise you display, the personal traits you show and the manner in which you respond.

ABOUT THIS BOOK

This book contains tests divided into Examination Sections. Go through each test, answering every question in the margin. We have also attached a sample answer sheet at the back of the book that can be removed and used. At the end of each test look at the answer key and check your answers. On the ones you got wrong, look at the right answer choice and learn. Do not fill in the answers first. Do not memorize the questions and answers, but understand the answer and principles involved. On your test, the questions will likely be different from the samples. Questions are changed and new ones added. If you understand these past questions you should have success with any changes that arise. Tests may consist of several types of questions. We have additional books on each subject should more study be advisable or necessary for you. Finally, the more you study, the better prepared you will be. This book is intended to be the last thing you study before you walk into the examination room. Prior study of relevant texts is also recommended. NLC publishes some of these in our Fundamental Series. Knowledge and good sense are important factors in passing your exam. Good luck also helps. So now study this Passbook, absorb the material contained within and take that knowledge into the examination. Then do your best to pass that exam.

EXAMINATION SECTION

EXAMINATION SECTION
TEST 1

DIRECTIONS: Each question or incomplete statement is followed by several suggested answers or completions. Select the one that BEST answers the question or completes the statement. *PRINT THE LETTER OF THE CORRECT ANSWER IN THE SPACE AT THE RIGHT.*

Questions 1-7.

DIRECTIONS: Questions 1 through 7 are to be answered on the basis of the following income statement.

Laura Lee's Bridal Shop
Income Statement
For the Year Ended December 31, 2018

Revenue:		
New & Used Bridal Gowns & Accessories		$55,000
Expenses:		
Advertisement Expense	$ 2,000	
Salaries Expense	12,000	
Dry cleaning & Alterations	10,000	
Utilities	1,500	
Total Expenses		25,500
Net Income		$29,500

1. What is the period of time covered by this income statement?   1.____

   A. January-December 2017
   B. December 2018
   C. January 2017-December 2018
   D. January-December 2018

2. What is the source of the revenue?   2.____

   A. New and used bridal gowns, advertisements, salaries, dry cleaning, and utilities
   B. Advertisements, salaries, dry cleaning, alterations, and utilities
   C. New and used bridal gowns and accessories
   D. Net income

3. What is the total revenue?   3.____

   A. $25,500   B. $55,000   C. $29,500   D. $79,500

4. Which of the following are expenses?   4.____

   A. Salaries
   B. New and used bridal gowns and accessories
   C. Revenue
   D. New and used bridal gowns, advertisements, and dry cleaning

5. What are the total expenses?   5.____

   A. $55,000   B. $29,500   C. $79,500   D. $25,500

6. There is a resulting net income because 6.____

   A. total revenue and total expenses are combined
   B. net income is greater than total revenue
   C. the total revenue is greater than total expenses
   D. the total revenue is less than total expenses

7. Is this statement an interim statement? 7.____

   A. *Yes*, because it covers an entire accounting period
   B. *No*, because it covers an entire accounting period
   C. *Yes*, because it covers a period of less than a year
   D. *No*, because it covers a period of more than a year

8. What is the name of the accounting report that may show either a net profit or a net loss for an accounting period? 8.____

   A. Income statement   B. Balance sheet
   C. Statement of capital   D. Classified balance sheet

9. What are the two main parts of the body of the income statement? 9.____

   A. Cash and Capital   B. Revenue and Expenses
   C. Liabilities and Capital   D. Assets and Notes Payable

10. If total revenue exceeds total expenses for an accounting period, what is the difference called? 10.____

    A. Gross income   B. Total liabilities
    C. Total assets   D. Net income

11. In the body of a balance sheet, what are the three sections called? 11.____

    A. Assets and liabilities
    B. Cash, liabilities, and revenue
    C. Assets, liabilities, and capital
    D. Revenue, assets, and capital

12. What business record shows the results of the proprietor's borrowing assets from the business, usually in anticipation of profits? 12.____

    A. Proprietor's withdrawals
    B. Accounts payable
    C. Liabilities and Capital
    D. Total liabilities

Questions 13-24.

DIRECTIONS: For each transaction given for Mona's Magic Moments Hair Salon in Questions 13 through 24, identify which journal the transaction should be recorded in.

13. April 1: Mona, the owner, paid the month's rent - $600.00; check no. 356. 13.____

    A. General   B. Cash disbursements
    C. Purchases   D. Sales

14. April 6: the salon purchased $300.00 worth of styling products on account from Pomme de Terre Company.

    A. Cash disbursements   B. General
    C. Sales   D. Purchases

14._____

15. April 8: sold $100.00 worth of hair products on account to Mrs. Angela Bray.

    A. Sales   B. Purchases
    C. Cash disbursements   D. General

15._____

16. April 11: the owner, Mona Ramen, withdrew $80.00 of styling products for personal use.

    A. Sales   B. Cash receipts
    C. General   D. Cash disbursements

16._____

17. April 13: paid Pomme de Terre Company $300.00 on account; check 357.

    A. Purchases   B. Cash disbursements
    C. Cash receipts   D. General

17._____

18. April 15: cash sales to date were $4,607.00.

    A. Cash disbursements   B. Purchases
    C. Sales   D. General

18._____

19. April 17: issued credit slip #17 to Mrs. Angela Bray for $25.00 for merchandise returned.

    A. Cash disbursements   B. Cash receipts
    C. Sales   D. General

19._____

20. April 19: paid electric bill for $250.00; check no. 358.

    A. Cash disbursements   B. Purchases
    C. General   D. Cash receipts

20._____

21. April 21: received $75.00 from Mrs. Angela Bray for balance due on account.

    A. Sales   B. Cash disbursements
    C. Cash receipts   D. Purchases

21._____

22. April 23: sold $88.00 of hair products on account to Ms. Tania Alioto.

    A. Purchases   B. Sales
    C. Cash disbursements   D. Cash receipts

22._____

23. April 27: purchased $500.00 of equipment from Salon Stylings Merchandisers on account.

    A. Cash disbursements   B. Sales
    C. General   D. Purchases

23._____

24. April 30: cash sales to date were $5023.00.

    A. Purchases   B. Sales
    C. Cash receipts   D. General

24._____

Questions 25-30.

DIRECTIONS: Questions 25 through 30 are to be answered on the basis of the following ledger for a barbecue take-out restaurant owned and operated by Ruby Joiner.

Cash		Accounts Receivable		Delivery Equipment	
450	150	360	170	5,000	
212	125	250	100	4,000	
328	440	165	120	3,000	
172	125	100	60		
250	70				
275	150				
325	50				

Supplies		Ruby Joiner, Capital		Accounts Payable	
40			8,200	10	600
65			2,000	15	300
30			2,097		200
25					

Ruby Joiner, Drawing		Advertising Expense		Delivery Income	
225		40			400
175		45			350
200					250
					100

Trucking Expense		Telephone Expense	
100		80	
50		40	
		20	

25. What is the balance on the Cash account shown above?

   A. 2,012.00   B. 1,110.00   C. 3,122.00   D. 902.00

26. What is the balance on the Accounts receivable account shown above?

   A. 425.00   B. 875.00   C. 450.00   D. 1315.00

27. What is the balance on the Accounts payable account shown above?

   A. 1100.00   B. 1075.00   C. 25.00   D. 1125.00

28. Which of the above accounts has a balance of 1100.00?

   A. Accounts payable   B. Delivery Income
   C. Cash   D. Delivery equipment

29. Which of the above accounts has a balance of 12,000.00?

   A. Ruby Joiner, Capital
   B. Cash and Accounts receivable combined
   C. Delivery equipment
   D. None of the accounts

30. If you made a balance sheet out of the information listed above, Ruby Joiner's total assets would be

   A. 14,472.00   B. 12,297.00   C. 13,392.00   D. 13,487.00

Questions 31-34.

DIRECTIONS: Questions 31 through 34 are to be answered on the basis of the following information, to be included on a checking deposit ticket.

Five $20 bills; 11 $10 bills; 6 $5 bills; 47 $1 bills; 200 half dollars; 120 quarters; 112 dimes; 320 nickels; 67 pennies. Second National Bank (73-124) check of 152.34; Bank of the Midwest (13-298) check of 68.37; Great National Bank (32-165) check of 185.06.

31. What is the TOTAL currency for this deposit? 31.____
   A. $387   B. $287   C. $444.87   D. $157.87

32. What is the TOTAL coin for this deposit? 32.____
   A. $387   B. $287   C. $444.87   D. $157.87

33. What is the check total for this deposit? 33.____
   A. $692.77   B. $406   C. $405.77   D. $850.64

34. What is the TOTAL deposit? 34.____
   A. $444.87   B. $692.77   C. $851   D. $850.64

Questions 35-37.

DIRECTIONS: Questions 35 through 37 are to be answered on the basis of the following petty cash journal.

Date	Receipt No.	To Whom Paid	For What	Acct.#	Amount
10/2	1	Anna Jones - Mail	Postage	548	13.50
10/2	2	Jim Collins	Messenger	525	5.75
10/4	3	Anna Jones - Mail	Postage	548	13.50
10/5	4	Lucky Stores	Coffee	515	7.34
10/6	5	Tom Allen	Lunch w/customer	525	11.38

35. What is the TOTAL disbursement from this fund for the time period 10/1 through 10/6? 35.____
   A. $51.47   B. $40.09   C. $61.47   D. $26.59

36. How much money was disbursed to Account #548 during the time period 10/1-10/16? 36.____
   A. $51.47   B. $26   C. $27   D. $34.34

37. If the fund began the month with a total of $100.00, what amount was left in the fund at the end of business on 10/5? 37.____
   A. $48.53   B. $59.91   C. $51.47   D. $40.09

Questions 38-40.

DIRECTIONS: Questions 38 through 40 are to be answered on the basis of the following information.

A promissory note dated December 1, 2018, bearing interest at a rate of 12% and due in 90 days, is sent to a creditor. The face value of the note is $900.

38. What is the due date of the promissory note?   38._____

    A. January 15, 2019   B. March 1, 2019
    C. February 1, 2019   D. December 31, 2018

39. What is the TOTAL interest that will be earned on the note?   39._____

    A. $27   B. $270   C. $108   D. $10.80

40. What interest will be earned on the note for the old accounting period (December 1-31)?   40._____

    A. $90   B. $36   C. $9   D. $3.60

KEY (CORRECT ANSWERS)

1.	D	11.	C	21.	C	31.	B
2.	C	12.	A	22.	B	32.	D
3.	B	13.	B	23.	D	33.	C
4.	A	14.	D	24.	B	34.	D
5.	D	15.	A	25.	D	35.	A
6.	C	16.	C	26.	A	36.	C
7.	B	17.	B	27.	B	37.	B
8.	A	18.	C	28.	B	38.	B
9.	B	19.	D	29.	C	39.	A
10.	D	20.	A	30.	D	40.	C

TEST 2

DIRECTIONS: Each question or incomplete statement is followed by several suggested answers or completions. Select the one that BEST answers the question or completes the statement. *PRINT THE LETTER OF THE CORRECT ANSWER IN THE SPACE AT THE RIGHT.*

Questions 1-4.

DIRECTIONS: Questions 1 through 4 are to be answered on the basis of the following information, to be included in a deposit slip.

    14 twenty dollar bills   63 quarters
    52 ten dollar bills   22 dimes
    12 five dollar bills   44 nickels
    43 one dollar bills   70 pennies

Checks: $236.34 and $129.72

1. What is the TOTAL amount of currency for this deposit?   1._____
   A. $923.85   B. $1269.06   C. $903.00   D. $1299.91

2. What is the TOTAL amount of coin for this deposit?   2._____
   A. $20.85   B. $923.85   C. $903.00   D. $1299.91

3. What is the TOTAL amount of check for this deposit?   3._____
   A. $20.85   B. $366.06   C. $1299.91   D. $903.00

4. What is the TOTAL deposit for this slip?   4._____
   A. $1269.06   B. $903.00   C. $923.85   D. $1289.91

Questions 5-7.

DIRECTIONS: Questions 5 through 7 are to be answered on the basis of the following information.

    Angela Martinez's last check stub balance was $675.50. Her bank statement balance dated April 30 was $652.00. A $250 deposit was in transit on that date. Outstanding checks were as follows: No. 127, $65.00; No. 129, $203.50; No. 130, $50.00. The bank service charge for the month was $5.00.

5. What was Angela Martinez's available checkbook balance on April 30?   5._____
   A. $652.00   B. $338.50   C. $583.50   D. $675.50

6. In order to reconcile her checkbook balance with her bank statement balance, what must Angela Martinez do?   6._____
   A. Add her checkbook balance to the balance on her bank statement
   B. Subtract her checkbook balance from the balance on her bank statement

C. Ignore her checkbook balance and adopt the balance on her bank statement
D. Adjust the checkbook balance by adding deposits and debiting outstanding checks and charges

7. The check stub balance referred to in the problem refers to the

A. last check Angela Martinez recorded in her checkbook
B. amount of money left in Angela Martinez's account according to her own calculations based on the checks, charges, and deposits she has written and recorded
C. amount of money left in Angela Martinez's account according to the bank's calculations based on the checks, charges, and deposits posted to her account
D. number of checks left in her checkbook

Questions 8-9.

DIRECTIONS: Questions 8 and 9 are to be answered on the basis of the following information.

Tu Nguyen, an interior designer, received his June bank statement on July 2. The balance was $622.66. His last check stub balance was $700. On comparing the two, he noticed that a deposit of $275 made on June 30 was not included on the statement; also, a bank service charge of $4 was deducted. Outstanding checks were as follows: No. 331, $97.50; No. 332, $207; No. 335, $25.40; and No. 336, $68.97.

8. What is Nguyen's CORRECT available bank balance?

A. $494.79   B. $897.66   C. $700.00   D. $219.79

9. The bank statement balance referred to in the problem refers to the

A. last check Tu Nguyen recorded in his checkbook
B. last check presented for payment to Tu Nguyen's account
C. amount of money left in Tu Nguyen's account according to the bank's calculations based on the checks, charges, and deposits posted to his account
D. amount of money left in Tu Nguyen's account based on his own calculations of the checks, charges, and deposits he has written and recorded

10. What of the following endorsements would be an example of a simple Endorsement in Blank?

A. Pay to the Order of Joanie Anderson
B. Joanie Anderson
C. For deposit only; Acct. No. 12345; Joanie Anderson
D. Without Recourse; Joanie Anderson

11. Which of the following endorsements would limit the further purpose or use of the endorsed check?

A. Pay to the Order of Joanie Anderson
B. Joanie Anderson
C. For deposit only; Acct. No. 12345; Joanie Anderson,
D. Without Recourse; Joanie Anderson

12. Which of the following endorsements would protect the endorser from legal responsibility for payment, should the drawer have insufficient funds to honor his/her own check?   12._____

    A. Pay to the Order of Joanie Anderson
    B. Joanie Anderson
    C. For deposit only; Acct. No. 12345; Joanie Anderson
    D. Without Recourse; Joanie Anderson

Questions 13-24.

DIRECTIONS: Questions 13 - 24 are to be answered on the basis of the following ledger accounts for Wheelsmith Organic Farms.

Wheelsmith Organic Farms
Ledger Accounts

Cash	Accounts Payable	Service Supplies
Jan. 1 4,000	Jan. 1 2,000	Jan. 1 2,000

Shelley Wheelsmith, Capital	Machinery
Jan. 1 11,000	Jan. 1 7,000

13. Transaction #1: On January 5, Shelley Wheelsmith, the proprietor, received cash amounting to $5,000 as a result of returning machinery that had recently been purchased. What account(s) should this transaction be posted to?   13._____

    A. Cash
    B. Cash and Machinery
    C. Machinery
    D. Cash, Machinery, and Service Supplies

14. Transaction #2: On January 8, Shelley Wheelsmith, the proprietor, sent out a check for $600 in partial payment of the accounts payable.
    What account(s) should this transaction be posted to?   14._____

    A. Accounts Payable
    B. Accounts Payable and Cash
    C. Accounts Payable and Capital
    D. Cash

15. Transaction #3: On January 14, Shelley Wheelsmith, proprietor, made an additional investment in the business by contributing machinery valued at $1,500. What account(s) should this transaction be posted to?   15._____

    A. Machinery   B. Machinery and Capital
    C. Capital   D. Machinery and Cash

16. Transaction #4: On January 26, Shelley Wheelsmith, proprietor, purchased additional service supplies for $200. She agreed to pay the obligation in 30 days. What account(s) should this transaction be posted to?   16._____

A. Accounts Payable and Liabilities
B. Service supplies
C. Accounts Payable
D. Accounts Payable and Service supplies

17. Transaction #5: On January 31, Shelley Wheelsmith, proprietor, purchased service supplies paying cash of $50. What account(s) should this transaction be posted to?   17._____

    A. Service supplies
    B. Service supplies and Accounts Payable
    C. Cash and Service supplies
    D. Cash

18. What is the balance in the Cash account after all of these transactions are posted?   18._____

    A. $9,000   B. $1,000   C. $5,000   D. $8,350

19. What is the balance in the Machinery account after all of these transactions are posted?   19._____

    A. $7,000   B. $5,000   C. $3,500   D. $13,500

20. What is the balance in the Accounts Payable account after all of these transactions are posted?   20._____

    A. $800   B. $600   C. $2,600   D. $1,600

21. What is the balance in the Capital account after all of these transactions are posted?   21._____

    A. $12,500   B. $800   C. $11,600   D. $10,400

22. What is the balance in the Service supplies account after all of these transactions are posted?   22._____

    A. $2,000   B. $2,250   C. $750   D. $2,200

23. What are the total assets of Wheelsmith Organic Farms after these transactions have been posted?   23._____

    A. $10,600   B. $11,850   C. $14,100   D. $10,750

24. What are the total liabilities and capital for Wheelsmith Organic Farms after these transactions have been posted?   24._____

    A. $14,100   B. $12,500   C. $11,850   D. $10,600

Questions 25-28.

DIRECTIONS: Questions 25 through 28 are to be answered on the basis of the following information.

At the end of an accounting period, Andy's Framing Gallery recorded the following information: Sales, $125,225; Merchandise Inventory, December 31, $95,325; Purchases Returns and Allowances, $3,500; Merchandise Inventory, January 1, $98,725; Freight on Purchases, $2,500; Purchases, $120,000.

25. What are the net purchases for Andy's Framing Gallery during the accounting period? 25.____
    A. $120,000   B. $119,000   C. $3,500   D. $122,500

26. What is the cost of goods available for sale? 26.____
    A. $119,000   B. $98,725   C. $95,325   D. $217,725

27. What is the total cost of goods sold for this accounting period? 27.____
    A. $217,725   B. $95,325   C. $122,400   D. $125,225

28. What is the gross profit on sales for this accounting period? 28.____
    A. $2825   B. $2500   C. $125,225   D. $122,400

Questions 29-40.

DIRECTIONS: Questions 29 through 40 are to be answered on the basis of the following information.

The Joie de Vivre Co. received the promissory notes listed below during the last quarter of its calendar year:

	Date	Face Amount	Terms	Interest Rate	Date Discounted	Discount Rate
(1)	10/8	$3,600	30 days	-	10/18	9%
(2)	9/22	$8,000	60 days	6%	10/1	7%
(3)	11/15	$3,000	90 days	7%	11/20	8%

29. What is the due date for the first note? 29.____
    A. 12/31   B. 11/7   C. 12/7   D. 10/31

30. What interest will be due when the first note matures? 30.____
    A. $3   B. $3,600   C. $30   D. $0

31. What is the maturity value of the first note? 31.____
    A. $3,600   B. $3,630   C. $0   D. $3,603

32. What is the discount period for the first note? 32.____
    A. One fiscal year   B. 10 days
    C. 20 days   D. One month

33. What is the due date for the second note? 33.____
    A. 12/21   B. 11/21   C. 10/21   D. 1/21

34. What interest will be due when the second note matures? 34.____
    A. $60   B. $800.00   C. $8.00   D. $80.00

35. What is the maturity value of the second note? 35.____
    A. $8,000   B. $8,080   C. $8,800   D. $8,008

36. What is the discount period for the second note? 36.____
    A. 51 days   B. 10 days   C. 360 days   D. 60 days

37. What is the due date for the third note? 37.____
    A. 1/14   B. 12/15   C. 12/31   D. 2/13

38. What interest will be due when the third note matures? 38.____
    A. $5.25   B. $52.50   C. $525   D. $90

39. What is the maturity value of the third note? 39.____
    A. $3525   B. $3005.25   C. $3052.50   D. $3090

40. What is the discount period for the third note? 40.____
    A. 60 days   B. 85 days   C. 5 days   D. 90 days

KEY (CORRECT ANSWERS)

1.	C	11.	C	21.	A	31.	A
2.	A	12.	D	22.	B	32.	C
3.	B	13.	B	23.	C	33.	B
4.	D	14.	B	24.	A	34.	D
5.	C	15.	B	25.	B	35.	B
6.	D	16.	D	26.	D	36.	A
7.	B	17.	C	27.	C	37.	D
8.	A	18.	D	28.	A	38.	B
9.	C	19.	C	29.	B	39.	C
10.	B	20.	D	30.	D	40.	B

TEST 3

DIRECTIONS: Each question or incomplete statement is followed by several suggested answers or completions. Select the one that BEST answers the question or completes the statement. *PRINT THE LETTER OF THE CORRECT ANSWER IN THE SPACE AT THE RIGHT.*

Questions 1-8.

DIRECTIONS: Questions 1 through 8 are to be answered on the basis of the following Balance Sheet.

Laura Lee's Bridal Shop
Balance Sheet
December 31, 2018

Assets
Cash	$14,000	
Accounts Receivable	3,000	
Bridal Accessories	10,000	
Gowns and Other Inventory	30,000	
Total Assets		$57,000

Liabilities and Capital
Accounts Payable	$ 4,000	
Notes Payable	28,000	
Total Liabilities		$32,000
Laura Lee, Capital		25,000
Total Liabilities and Capital		$57,000

1. When was the balance sheet prepared?   1._____

   A. January 2019
   B. December 31, 2018
   C. After the close of the 2018 fiscal year
   D. December 1, 2018

2. How does the date on this balance sheet differ from the date on the statement of capital or income statement?   2._____

   A. It doesn't differ. The dates for each statement signify the same time period.
   B. The date on a balance sheet represents the period during which any changes indicated on the statement took place, whereas the other financial statements represent the moment in time when the statement was prepared.
   C. The date on a balance sheet represents the moment in time when the statement was prepared, whereas the other financial statements represent the period during which any changes indicated on the statement took place.
   D. The date on a balance sheet indicates an entire year, whereas the dates on the other statements indicate a single month.

3. Can Laura Lee purchase more bridal gowns for the business paying cash of $16,000?   3._____

   A. *No*, because the business has only $14,000 cash available
   B. *Yes*, because the business has $57,000 cash available
   C. *Yes*, because the business has $57,000 available in assets
   D. *No*, because the business has $57,000 in liabilities

13

4. What is the owner's equity of Laura Lee's Bridal Shop? 4._____
 Since total equity consists of total _____, total equity is _____.

 A. assets minus total liabilities and proprietor's capital; $0
 B. assets minus total liabilities; $25,000
 C. assets; $57,000
 D. liabilities and proprietor's capital; $57,000

5. What is the TOTAL amount of Laura Lee's claim against the total assets of the business? 5._____

 A. $57,000   B. $25,000   C. $0   D. $39,000

6. What is the amount of the creditors' claims against the assets of the business? 6._____

 A. $4,000   B. $57,000   C. $32,000   D. $28,000

7. What is the net income for the period? 7._____

 A. $57,000
 B. $0
 C. $25,000
 D. This information cannot be obtained from the balance sheet

8. What was the value of Laura Lee's ownership in this business on January 1, 2004? 8._____

 A. $25,000
 B. $57,000
 C. $14,000
 D. This information cannot be obtained from the balance sheet

Questions 9-21.

DIRECTIONS: Each of the transactions described in Questions 9 through 21 occurred within an accounting period. For each question, indicate which of the four journals the transaction would be recorded in.

9. Sale of goods on account 9._____

 A. Cash receipts   B. Cash payments
 C. General   D. Sales

10. Cash payment of a promissory note 10._____

 A. Cash payments   B. Cash receipts
 C. Sales   D. General

11. Received a credit memo from a creditor 11._____

 A. Purchases   B. General
 C. Sales   D. Cash payments

12. Sale of merchandise for cash 12._____

 A. Purchases   B. General
 C. Cash receipts   D. Cash payments

13. Received a check from a customer in partial payment of an oral agreement 13.____

    A. Purchases B. Sales
    C. General   D. Cash receipts

14. Issued a credit memo to a customer 14.____

    A. Purchases   B. General
    C. Cash payments D. Sales

15. Received a promissory note in place of an oral agreement from a customer 15.____

    A. General   B. Cash payments
    C. Cash receipts D. Sales

16. Paid monthly rent 16.____

    A. General   B. Purchases
    C. Cash payments D. Cash receipts

17. Sale of a service on credit 17.____

    A. Cash receipts B. General
    C. Purchases   D. Sales

18. Purchase of office furniture on credit 18.____

    A. General   B. Purchases
    C. Cash payments D. Cash receipts

19. Purchased merchandise for cash 19.____

    A. Cash payments B. Cash receipts
    C. Sales   D. General

20. Cash refund to a customer 20.____

    A. Cash receipts B. Sales
    C. General   D. Cash payments

21. Purchases made on credit 21.____

    A. Purchases   B. Sales
    C. Cash receipts D. General

Questions 22-26.

DIRECTIONS: Questions 22 through 26 are to be answered on the basis of the following inventory, purchased by International Soap and Candle Traders, Inc.

700 units at $4.50, 320 units at $3.75, 550 units at $2.75, and 475 units at $1.90

22. Calculate the total price of the units that cost $4.50. 22.____

    A. $315   B. $31,500   C. $3,150   D. $2,800

23. Calculate the total price of the units that cost $3.75. 23.____

    A. $2062.50   B. $12,000   C. $120   D. $1,200

24. Calculate the total price of the units that cost $2.75.

    A. $1,512.50   B. $15,125   C. $151.25   D. $550

25. Calculate the total price of the units that cost $1.90.

    A. $90.25   B. $9025   C. $902.50   D. $475

26. Calculate the average cost per unit.

    A. $27   B. $33.10   C. $0.30   D. $3.31

27. The interest on a promissory note is recorded at which of the following times?

    A. When the debt is incurred
    B. At the end of the accounting period
    C. When the note is paid
    D. At the beginning of each month

28. The interest on a promissory note begins accruing at which of the following times?

    A. When the debt is incurred
    B. At the end of the accounting period
    C. When the note is paid
    D. At the beginning of each month

29. The maturity value of an interest-bearing note is the

    A. interest accrued on the note plus a service charge imposed by the lender
    B. interest accrued on the note
    C. face value of the note
    D. principal of the note plus interest

30. A cash receipts journal is used to record the

    A. number of cash sales a business makes
    B. number of credit sales a business makes
    C. collection of cash made by the business
    D. expenditure of cash made by the business

31. Calculate the interest on a promissory note issued for $3,000 at an interest rate of 8%, due in 360 days. (Assume a banking year of 360 days.)

    A. $300   B. $240   C. $60   D. $360

32. Calculate the total payment due for a promissory note issued for $1,000 at an interest rate of 10%, due in 90 days. (Assume a banking year of 360 days.)

    A. $25   B. $1050   C. $1000   D. $1025

33. Calculate the total payment due for a promissory note issued for $5,000 at an interest rate of 6%, due in 60 days. (Assume a banking year of 360 days.)

    A. $5,050   B. $50   C. $5,000   D. $5,300

34. Calculate the interest on a promissory note issued for $1,700 at an interest rate of 12%, due in 45 days. (Assume a banking year of 360 days.)   34.____

   A. $204   B. $1725.50   C. $25.50   D. $1904

35. Calculate the interest on a promissory note issued for $600 at an interest rate of 9%, due in 90 days. (Assume a banking year of 360 days.)   35.____

   A. $13.50   B. $135   C. $54   D. $540

KEY (CORRECT ANSWERS)

1. B		16. C	
2. C		17. D	
3. A		18. B	
4. B		19. A	
5. B		20. D	
6. C		21. A	
7. D		22. C	
8. D		23. D	
9. D		24. A	
10. A		25. C	
11. B		26. D	
12. C		27. C	
13. D		28. A	
14. B		29. D	
15. A		30. C	

31. B
32. D
33. A
34. C
35. A

CLERICAL ABILITIES TESTS

This guide provides a general description of the subject areas to be tested and the different types of questions you will likely see on any of the tests in this series. The Examination Announcement will specify the exact subject areas to be included on the specific test you will be taking.

The Clerical Abilities Tests have an overall time allowance of 3 hours. They are divided into five subject areas and the questions are designed to evaluate the following abilities:

1. SPELLING: These questions test your ability to spell words that are used in written business communications.
2. ALPHABETIZING: These questions test your ability to file material in alphabetical order.
3. RECORD KEEPING: These questions evaluate your ability to perform common record keeping tasks. The test consists of two or more "sets" of questions; each set concerning a different problem. Typical record keeping problems might involve the organization or collation of data from several sources; scheduling; maintaining a record system using running balances; or completion of a table summarizing data using totals, subtotals, averages and percents.
4. CLERICAL OPERATIONS WITH LETTERS AND NUMBERS: These questions test your skills and abilities in clerical operations involving alphabetizing, comparing, checking and counting. The questions require you to follow the specific directions given for each question which may involve alphabetizing, comparing, checking and counting given groups of letters and/or numbers.
5. USING A DIRECTORY: These questions test your ability to keep directory records and to supply accurate information to callers. The questions require you to incorporate name and/or room changes into a current telephone directory and to answer questions, such as those that would be asked by callers, about the information contained in the directory listing.

The Examination Announcement will list two or more of the above subject areas to be included in the written test you will be taking. All written tests in the series include CLERICAL OPERATIONS WITH LETTERS AND NUMBERS.

The remainder of this guide explains how you are tested in each of these subject areas. A **TEST TASK** is provided for each subject. This is an explanation of how a question is presented and how to correctly answer it. Be sure to read each one carefully.

You will also be given at least one **SAMPLE QUESTION** for each subject area. It will be of the type that you will see on the actual test. The **SOLUTION** and correct answer are provided after each question. You should study the question and its solution until you understand how it works.

SUBJECT AREA 1

SPELLING: These questions test you ability to spell words that are used in written business communications.

TEST TASK: You are given questions that contain a list of words. You must determine which, if any, of the words is misspelled.

SAMPLE QUESTION:

> Which one of the following words is misspelled?
> A. manageable
> B. circumstants
> C. legality
> D. None of the above is misspelled

The answer is B.

SOLUTION: *To answer this question, you must examine each of the words. The words "manageable" (choice A) and "legality" (choice C) are spelled correctly. The word "circumstants" (choice B) is misspelled. The correct spelling is "circumstance."*

SUBJECT AREA 2

ALPHABETIZING: These questions test your ability to file material in alphabetical order.

TEST TASK: You will be provided with a list of names. You must put the names into alphabetical order.

SAMPLE QUESTION:

> Of the following, which one should be THIRD in an alphabetical file?
> A. Docker, John
> B. Decker, Jane
> C. Dinckman, June
> D. Dockman, James

The answer is A.

SOLUTION: *To answer this question, you must first put the names into alphabetical order. "Decker, Jane" would be first. "Dinckman, June" would be second. "Docker, John" would be third followed by "Dockman, James." The question asks for the third name on the list. The answer is "Docker, John" (choice A).*

SUBJECT AREA 3

RECORD KEEPING: These questions test your ability to perform common record keeping tasks.

TEST TASK: The questions in this subject area are contained in two or more sets. Each set presents a different problem. Typical record keeping problems might involve:
- organization or collation of data from several sources
- scheduling
- maintaining a record system using running balances
- completion of a table summarizing data using totals, subtotals, averages and percents

SAMPLE QUESTIONS:

The following two questions are based on the table below.

NUMBER OF AUTOMOBILE ACCIDENTS BY LOCATION AND CAUSE (1998)				
	LOCATION 1		LOCATION 2	
CAUSE	Number	Percent	Number	Percent
Road Conditions	10	20	25	42
Drunk Drivers	20	40	5	8
Speeding	15	30	15	25
Unknown	5	10	15	25
TOTALS	50	100	60	100

QUESTION 1: Which of the following is the SECOND highest cause of accidents for both locations combined?
- A. Road Conditions
- B. Drunk Drivers
- C. Speeding
- D. Unknown

The answer is C

SOLUTION: To answer this question, you must first add the number from location 1 to the number from location 2 for each accident cause. Then, you must rank the causes from highest to lowest based on the totals you obtain. You can then determine the second highest cause of accidents for both locations combined. In this example, "Road Conditions" (choice A) would be the highest cause of accidents with 35. The second highest cause of accidents is "Speeding" (choice C) with 30. The correct answer is "Speeding" (choice C).

QUESTION 2: The average number of automobile accidents per week that occurred in Location 2 in 1998 (52 weeks) was most nearly
- A. 0.8
- B. 1.2
- C. 2.1
- D. 5.2

The answer is B

SOLUTION: To answer this question, you must divide the total number of accidents in location 2 (60), by 52 weeks. The answer, rounded to the nearest tenth is 1.2 (choice B).

SUBJECT AREA 4

CLERICAL OPERATIONS WITH LETTERS AND NUMBERS: These questions test your skills and abilities in clerical operations involving alphabetizing, comparing, checking and counting. The questions require you to follow the specific directions given for each question which may involve alphabetizing, comparing, checking and counting given groups of letters and/or numbers.

TEST TASK: You are given questions, which require you to follow specific directions given for each question. Each question may involve alphabetizing, comparing, checking and counting given groups of letters and/or numbers.

SAMPLE QUESTIONS:

QUESTION 1: How many pairs of the following groups of letters are exactly alike?

BRFQSX   BRFQSX
ACDOBJ   ACDBOJ
RPTQVS   RPTQVS
ZUYRVB   ZUYRVB
SPQRAS   SQRPAS
HVCBWR   HVCRWB

A. 2
B. 3
C. 4
D. 5

The answer is B.

SOLUTION: *To answer this question you must compare the column of letter groups on the left to the column of letter groups on the right. BRFQSX, RPTQVS and ZUYRVB of the left column are exactly like BRFQSX, RPTQVS and ZUYRVB of the right column. The other groups of letters are not exactly alike so the answer is 3 (choice B).*

QUESTION 2: In the following sentence, how many words contain letters that appear more than once in that word?

"Right around April Fool's Day, the daffodils and crocuses start to emerge and cheer us up after a long winter."

A. 5
B. 6
C. 7
D. 8

The answer is B.

SOLUTION: *To answer this question, look at each word to see how many contain the same letter at least twice. The words that do are: "Fool's," "daffodils," "crocuses," "start," "emerge," and "cheer." The total number of words is 6. The answer is 6 (choice B).*

SUBJECT AREA 4 (cont.)

QUESTION 3: Which one of the following letters is as far after C as T is after O in the alphabet?

A. G
B. H
C. I
D. J

The answer is B.

SOLUTION: *Count how many letters are between O and T in the alphabet. There are 4: P, Q, R and S. There are also 4 letters between C and H: D, E, F and G. The answer is H (choice B).*

QUESTION 4: In the following list of numbers, how many times does 8 come just after 6 when 6 comes just after an odd number?

63256872534942368445768423968686

A. 2
B. 3
C. 4
D. 5

The answer is C.

SOLUTION: *To answer this question, you must determine the number of times 8 follows 6 when 6 follows an odd number. There are 4 occasions where 8 follows 6 and the number 6 follows an odd number. They are 568, 368, 768 and 968. The answer is 4 (choice C).*

SUBJECT AREA 5

USING A DIRECTORY: These questions test your ability to keep directory records and to supply accurate information to callers.

TEST TASK: You will be provided with a telephone directory and a list of changes, and you will be asked to incorporate name and/or room changes into the directory. You will be asked to answer questions such as those that would be asked by callers about the information contained in the directory listing.

SAMPLE QUESTION:

Example: This question is based on the DIRECTORY and LIST OF CHANGES shown below:

DIRECTORY

NAME	RM. NO.	EXT.	NAME	RM. NO.	EXT.
Adams, Dave	123	1234	Charles, Bob	126	9109
Brown, Bill	125	5678	Davis, Ann	128	1112
Brull, Betty	142	5768	Diaz, Angel	134	2212
Calvin, Ed	155	2314	Evans, Sue	127	9502
Cerra, Lisa	116	4312	Frank, Chris	151	3456

LIST OF CHANGES in effect today:

All calls for persons not listed above should be referred to Ann Davis in Personnel.

Bill Brown is on vacation; his calls should be referred to Dave Adams whose extension has been changed to 8737.

QUESTION: To which one of the following extensions should a call for Marc Evans be directed?

A. 1112
B. 1234
C. 5678
D. 8737

Answer is A.

SOLUTION: *To answer this question, you must first determine that Marc Adams is not listed in the directory above, and that calls for people not so listed should be referred to Ann Davis in Personnel. Find Ann Davis in the directory; her extension is 1112 (choice A).*

CONCLUSION

You and your feelings about tests have a great deal to do with how you perform on a test. Some people get so tense and nervous that they don't do as well as they could. They forget things they know or make simple mistakes. The following suggestions should help you overcome these problems.

- Study and review this Guide to become familiar with the test contents.
- Give yourself plenty of time to do what you need to do before the test starts. Arrive at the test room a little ahead of the starting time.
- Try to relax just before the test starts.
- Listen carefully to the instructions the Monitors give you. Carefully read all instructions on the Candidate Directions you are given at the test as well as information on the covers of the test booklets.
- Try to keep calm, cool and collected throughout the test.
- Keep track of time.

CLERICAL ABILITIES TEST

Clerical aptitude involves the ability to perceive pertinent detail in verbal or tabular material, to observe differences in copy, to proofread words and numbers, and to avoid perceptual errors in arithmetic computation.

NATURE OF THE TEST

Four types of clerical aptitude questions are presented in the Clerical Abilities Test. There are 120 questions with a short time limit. The test contains 30 questions on name and number checking, 30 on the arrangement of names in correct alphabetical order, 30 on simple arithmetic, and 30 on inspecting groups of letters and numbers. The questions have been arranged in groups or cycles of five questions of each type. The Clerical Abilities Test is primarily a test of speed in carrying out relatively simple clerical tasks. While accuracy on these tasks is important and will be taken into account in the scoring, experience has shown that many persons are so concerned about accuracy that they do the test more slowly than they should. Competitors should be cautioned that speed as well as accuracy is important to achieve a good score.

HOW THE TEST IS ADMINISTERED

Each competitor should be given a copy of the test booklet with sample questions on the cover page, an answer sheet, and a medium No. 2 pencil. Ten minutes are allowed to study the directions and sample questions and to answer the questions in the proper boxes on the two pages.
The separate answer sheet should be used for the test proper. Fifteen minutes are allowed for the test.

HOW THE TEST IS SCORED

The correct answers should be counted and recorded. The number of incorrect answers must also be counted because one-fourth of the number of incorrect answers is subtracted from the number of right answers. An omission is considered as neither a right nor a wrong answer. The score on this test is the number of right answers minus one-fourth of the number of wrong answers (fractions of one-half or less are dropped). For example, if an applicant had answered 89 questions correctly and 10 questions incorrectly, and had omitted 1 question, his score would be 87.

28

EXAMINATION SECTION

DIRECTIONS: This test contains four kinds of questions. There are some of each kind on each page in the booklet. The time limit for the test will be announced by the examiner.
Use the special pencil furnished by the examiner in marking your answers on the separate answer sheet. For each question, there are five suggested answers. Decide which answer is correct, find the number of the question on the answer sheet, and make a solid black mark between the dotted lines just below the letter of your answer. If you wish to change your answer, erase the first mark completely, do not merely cross it out.

SAMPLE QUESTIONS

In each line across the page there are three names or numbers that are much alike. Compare the three names or numbers and decide which ones are exactly alike. On the Sample Answer Sheet at the right, mark the answer
- A. if ALL THREE names or numbers are exactly ALIKE
- B. if only the FIRST and SECOND names or numbers are exactly ALIKE
- C. if only the FIRST and THIRD names or numbers are exactly ALIKE
- D. if only the SECOND and THIRD names or numbers are exactly ALIKE
- E. if ALL THREE names or numbers are DIFFERENT

I.	Davis Hazen	David Hozen	David Hazen
II.	Lois Appel	Lois Appel	Lois Apfel
III.	June Allan	Jane Allan	Jane Allan
IV.	10235	10235	10235
V.	32614	32164	32614

It will be to your advantage to learn what A, B, C, D, and E stand for. If you finish the sample questions before you are told to turn to the test, study them.

In the next group of sample questions, there is a name in a box at the left, and four other names in alphabetical order at the right. Find the correct space for the boxed name so that it will be in alphabetical order with the others, and mark the letter of that space as your answer.

VI. [Jones, Jane]
   A. →
      Goodyear, G.L.
   B. →
      Haddon, Harry
   C. →
      Jackson, Mary
   D. →
      Jenkins, William
   E. →

VII. [Kessler, Neilson]
   A. →
      Kessel, Carl
   B. →
      Kessinger, D.J.
   C. →
      Kessler, Karl
   D. →
      Kessner, Lewis
   E. →

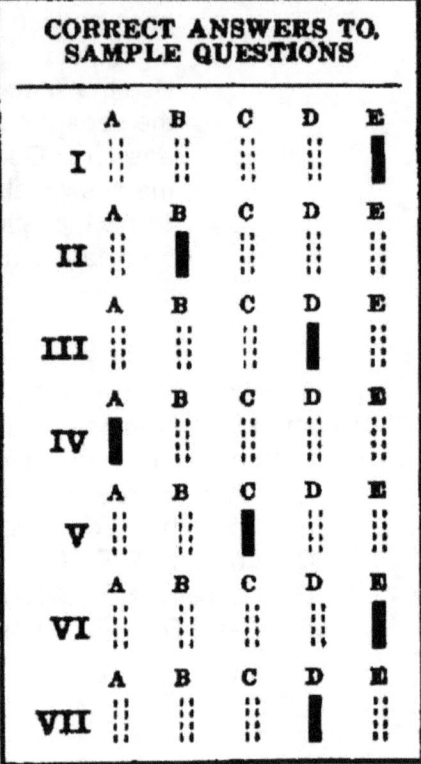

DIRECTIONS: In the following questions, complete the equation and find your answer among the list of suggested answers. Mark the Sample Answer Sheet A, B, C, or D for the answer you obtained; or if your answer is not among these, mark E for that question.

VIII. Add: 22
            +33

   A. 44   B. 45   C. 54   D. 55   E. None of these

IX. Subtract: 24
              - 3

   A. 20   B. 21   C. 27   D. 29   E. None of these

X. Multiply: 25
             x 5

   A. 100   B. 115   C. 125   D. 135   E. None of these

XI. Divide: 6/126

  A. 20   B. 22   C. 24   D. 26   E. None of these

DIRECTIONS: There is one set of suggested answers for the next group of sample questions. Do not try to memorize these answers, because there will be a different set on each age in the test.

To find the answer to a question, find which suggested answer contains numbers and letters, all of which appear in the question. If no suggested answer fits, mark E for that question.

XII. 8 N K 9 G T 4 6

XIII. T 9 7 Z 6 L 3 K

XIV. Z 7 G K 3 9 8 N

XV. 3 K 9 4 6 G Z L

XVI. Z N 7 3 8 K T 9

Suggested Answers
A = 7, 9, G, K
B = 8, 9, T, Z
C = 6, 7, K, Z
D = 6, 8, G, T
E = None of the above

After you have marked your answers to all the questions on the Sample Answer Sheets on this page and on the front page of the booklet, check them with the answers in the boxes marked Correct Answers To Sample Questions.

Questions 1-5.

In Questions 1 through 5, compare the three names or numbers, and mark
  A. if ALL THREE names or numbers are exactly ALIKE
  B. if only the FIRST and SECOND names or numbers are exactly ALIKE
  C. if only the FIRST and THIRD names or numbers are exactly ALIKE
  D. if only the SECOND and THIRD names or numbers are exactly ALIKE
  E. if ALL THREE names or numbers are DIFFERENT

1. 5261383   5261383   5261338

2. 8125690   8126690   8125609

3. W.E. Johnston   W.E. Johnson   W.E. Johnson

4. Vergil L. Muller   Vergil L. Muller   Vergil L. Muller

5. Atherton R. Warde   Asheton R. Warde   Atherton P. Warde

Questions 6-10.

In Questions 6 through 10, find the correct place for the name in the box

6. | Hackett, Gerald |

A. →
   Habert, James
B. →
   Hachett, J.J.
C. →
   Hachetts, K. Larson
D. →
   Hachettson, Leroy
E. →

7. | Margenroth, Alvin |

A. →
   Margeroth, Albert
B. →
   Margestein, Dan
C. →
   Margestein, David
D. →
   Margue, Edgar
E. →

8. | Bobbitt, Olivier E. |

A. →
   Bobbitt, D. Olivier
B. →
   Bobbitt, Olivia B
C. →
   Bobbitt, Olivia H.
D. →
   Bobbitt, R. Olivia
E. →

9. | Mosley, Werner |

A. →
   Mosely, Albert J.
B. →
   Mosley, Alvin
C. →
   Mosley, S.M.
D. →
   Mozley, Vinson N.
E. →

10. Youmuns, Frank L.

A. →
   Youmons, Frank G.
B. →
   Youmons, Frank H.
C. →
   Youmons, Frank K.
D. →
   Youmons, Frank M.
E. →

Questions 11-15.

11. Add: 43
        +32

    A. 55   B. 65   C. 66   D. 75   E. None of these

12. Subtract: 83
             - 4

    A. 73   B. 79   C. 80   D. 89   E. None of these

13. Multiply: 41
             x 7

    A. 281   B. 287   C. 291   D. 297   E. None of these

14. Divide: 6/306

    A. 44   B. 51   C. 52   D. 60   E. None of these

15. Add: 37
        +15

    A. 42   B. 52   C. 53   D. 62   E. None of these

Questions 16-20.

In Questions 16 through 20, find which one of the suggested answers appears in that question.

16. 6 2 5 K 4 P T G

17. L 4 7 2 T 6 V K

18. 3 5 4 L 9 V T G

19. G 4 K 7 L 3 5 Z

SUGGESTED ANSWERS
A = 4, 5, K, T
B = 4, 7, G, K
C = 2, 5, G, L
D = 2, 7, L, T
E = None of the above

20. 4 K 2 9 N 5 T G

Questions 21-25.

In Questions 21 through 25, compare the three names or numbers, and mark
    A. if ALL THREE names or numbers are exactly ALIKE
    B. if only the FIRST and SECOND names or numbers are exactly ALIKE
    C. if only the FIRST and THIRD names or numbers are exactly ALIKE
    D. if only the SECOND and THIRD names or numbers are exactly ALIKE
    E. if ALL THREE names or numbers are DIFFERENT

21. 2395890   2395890   2395890

22. 1926341   1926347   1926314

23. E. Owens McVey   E. Owen McVey   E. Owen McVay

24. Emily Neal Rouse   Emily Neal Rowse   Emily Neal Rowse

25. H. Merritt Audubon   H. Merriott Audubon H. Merritt Audubon

Questions 26-30.

In Questions 26 through 30, find the correct place for the name in the box.

26. | Watters, N.O. |
    A. →
       Waters, Charles L.
    B. →
       Waterson, Nina P.
    C. →
       Watson, Nora J.
    D. →
       Wattwood, Paul A.
    E. →

27. | Johnston, Edward |
    A. →
       Johnston, Edgar R.
    B. →
       Johnston, Edmond
    C. →
       Johnston, Edmund
    D. →
       Johnstone, Edmund A.
    E. →

28. Rensch, Adeline
    A. →
       Ramsay, Amos
    B. →
       Remschel, Augusta
    C. →
       Renshaw, Austin
    D. →
       Rentzel, Becky
    E. →

29. Schnyder, Maurice
    A. →
       Schneider, Martin
    B. →
       Schneider, Mertens
    C. →
       Schnyder, Newman
    D. →
       Schreibner, Norman
    E. →

30. Freedenburg, C. Erma
    A. →
       Freedenberg, Emerson
    B. →
       Freedenberg, Erma
    C. →
       Freedenberg, Erma E.
    D. →
       Freedinberg, Erma F.
    E. →

Questions 31-35.

31. Subtract: 68
             - 47

    A. 10   B. 11   C. 20   D. 22   E. None of these

32. Multiply: 50
              x 8

    A. 400   B. 408   C. 450   D. 458   E. None of these

33. Divide: 9/180

    A. 20   B. 29   C. 30   D. 39   E. None of these

34. Add: 78
          + 63

    A. 131   B. 140   C. 141   D. 151   E. None of these

35. Add: 89
         -70

   A. 9   B. 18   C. 19   D. 29   E. None of these

Questions 36-40.

In Questions 36 through 40, find which one of the suggested answers appears in that question.

36. 9 G Z 3 L 4 6 N

37. L 5 N K 4 3 9 V

38. 8 2 V P 9 L Z 5

39. V P 9 Z 5 L 8 7

40. 5 T 8 N 2 9 V L

SUGGESTED ANSWERS
A = 4, 9, L, V
B = 4, 5, N, Z
C = 5, 8, L, Z
D = 8, 9, N, V
E = None of the above

Questions 41-45.

In Questions 41 through 45, compare the three names or numbers, and mark
   A. if ALL THREE names or numbers are exactly ALIKE
   B. if only the FIRST and SECOND names or numbers are exactly ALIKE
   C. if only the FIRST and THIRD names or numbers are exactly ALIKE
   D. if only the SECOND and THIRD names or numbers are exactly ALIKE
   E. if ALL THREE names or numbers are DIFFERENT

41. 6219354	621354	6219354
42. 2312793	2312793	2312793
43. 1065407	1065407	1065047
44. Francis Ransdell	Frances Ramsdell	Francis Ramsdell
45. Cornelius Detwiler	Cornelius Detwiler	Cornelius Detwiler

Questions 46-50.

In Questions 46 through 50, find the correct place for the name in the box.

46. | DeMattia, Jessica |

    A. →
       DeLong, Jesse
    B. →
       DeMatteo, Jessie
    C. →
       Derby, Jessie S.
    D. →
       DeShazo, L.M.
    E. →

47. | Theriault, Louis |

    A. →
       Therien, Annette
    B. →
       Therien, Elaine
    C. →
       Thibeault, Gerald
    D. →
       Thiebeault, Pierre
    E. →

48. | Gaston, M. Hubert |

    A. →
       Gaston, Dorothy M.
    B. →
       Gaston, Henry N.
    C. →
       Gaston, Isabel
    D. →
       Gaston, M. Melvin
    E. →

49. | SanMiguel, Carlos |

    A. →
       SanLuis, Juana
    B. →
       Santilli, Laura
    C. →
       Stinnett, Nellie
    D. →
       Stoddard, Victor
    E. →

50. | DeLaTour, Hall F. |

A. →
   DeLargy, Harold
B. →
   DeLathouder, Hilda
C. →
   Lathrop, Hillary
D. →
   LaTour, Hulbert E.
E. →

Questions 51-55.

51. Multiply: 62
    × 5

    A. 300   B. 310   C. 315   D. 360   E. None of these

52. Divide: 3/153

    A. 41   B. 43   C. 51   D. 53   E. None of these

53. Add: 47
    +21

    A. 58   B. 59   C. 67   D. 68   E. None of these

54. Subtract: 87
    − 42

    A. 34   B. 35   C. 44   D. 45   E. None of these

55. Multiply: 37
    × 3

    A. 91   B. 101   C. 104   D. 114   E. None of these

Questions 56-60.

For Questions 56 through 60, find which one of the suggested answers appears in that question.

56. N 5 4 7 T K 3 Z

57. 8 5 3 V L 2 Z N

58. 7 2 5 N 9 K L V

59. 9 8 L 2 5 Z K V

60. Z 6 5 V 9 3 P N

SUGGESTED ANSWERS
A = 3, 8, K, N
B = 5, 8, N, V
C = 3, 9, V, Z
D = 5, 9, K, Z
E = None of the above

Questions 61-65.

In Questions 61 through 65, compare the three names or numbers, and mark
- A. if ALL THREE names or numbers are exactly ALIKE
- B. if only the FIRST and SECOND names or numbers are exactly ALIKE
- C. if only the FIRST and THIRD names or numbers are exactly ALIKE
- D. if only the SECOND and THIRD names or numbers are exactly ALIKE
- E. if ALL THREE names or numbers are DIFFERENT

61.	6452054	6452654	6452054
62.	8501268	8501268	8501286
63	Ella Burk Newham	Ella Burk Newnham	Elena Burk Newnham
64.	Jno. K. Ravencroft	Jno. H. Ravencroft	Jno. H. Ravencoft
65.	Martin Wills Pullen	Martin Wills Pulen	Martin Wills Pullen

Questions 66-70.

In Questions 66 through 70, find the correct place for the name in the box.

66. | O'Bannon, M.J. |

A. →
O'Beirne, B.B.
B. →
Oberlin, E.L.
C. →
Oberneir, L.P.
D. →
O'Brian, S.F.
E. →

67. | Entsminger, Jacob |

A. →
Ensminger, J.
B. →
Entsminger, J.A.
C. →
Entsminger, Jack
D. →
Entsminger, James
E. →

68. Iacone, Pete R.
   A. →
      Iacone, Pedro
   B. →
      Iacone, Pedro M.
   C. →
      Iacone, Peter F.
   D. →
      Iascone, Peter W.
   E. →

69. Sheppard, Gladys
   A. →
      Shepard, Dwight
   B. →
      Shepard, F.H.
   C. →
      Shephard, Louise
   D. →
      Shepperd, Stella
   E. →

70. Thackton, Melvin T.
   A. →
      Thackston, Milton G.
   B. →
      Thackston, Milton W.
   C. →
      Thackston, Theodore
   D. →
      Thackston, Thomas G.
   E. →

Questions 71-75.

71. Divide: 7/357

    A. 51   B. 52   C. 53   D. 54   E. None of these

72. Add: 58
        +27

    A. 75   B. 84   C. 85   D. 95   E. None of these

73. Subtract: 86
              - 57

    A. 18   B. 29   C. 38   D. 39   E. None of these

40

74. Multiply: 68
    x 4

   A. 242   B. 264   C. 272   D. 274   E. None of these

75. Divide: 9/639̄

   A. 71   B. 73   C. 81   D. 83   E. None of these

Questions 76-80.

For Questions 76 through 80, find which one of the suggested answers appears in that question.

76. 6 Z T N 8 7 4 V

77. V 7 8 6 N 5 P L

78. N 7 P V 8 4 2 L

79. 7 8 G 4 3 V L T

80. 4 8 G 2 T N 6 L

SUGGESTED ANSWERS
A = 2, 7, L, N
B = 2, 8, T, V
C = 6, 8, L, T
D = 6, 7, N, V
E = None of the above

Questions 81-85.

In Questions 81 through 85, compare the three names or numbers, and mark
   A. if ALL THREE names or numbers are exactly ALIKE
   B. if only the FIRST and SECOND names or numbers are exactly ALIKE
   C. if only the FIRST and THIRD names or numbers are exactly ALIKE
   D. if only the SECOND and THIRD names or numbers are exactly ALIKE
   E. if ALL THREE names or numbers are DIFFERENT

81. 3457988   3457986   3457986

82. 4695682   4695862   4695682

83. Stricklund Kanedy   Stricklund Kanedy   Stricklund Kanedy

84. Joy Harbor Witner   Joy Harloe Witner   Joy Harloe Witner

85. R.M.O. Uberroth   R.M.O. Uberroth   R.N.O. Uberroth

Questions 86-90.

In Questions 86 through 90, find the correct place for the name in the box.

86. Dunlavey, M. Hilary

A. →
Dunleavy, Hilary G.
B. →
Dunleavy, Hilary K.
C. →
Dunleavy, Hilary S.
D. →
Dunleavy, Hilery W.
E. →

87. Yarbrough, Maria

A. →
Yabroudy, Margy
B. →
Yarboro, Marie
C. →
Yarborough, Marina
D. →
Yarborough, Mary
E. →

88. Prouty, Martha

A. →
Proutey, Margaret
B. →
Proutey, Maude
C. →
Prouty, Myra
D. →
Prouty, Naomi
E. →

89. Pawlowicz, Ruth M.

A. →
Pawalek, Edward
B. →
Pawelek, Flora G.
C. →
Pawlowski, Joan M.
D. →
Pawtowski, Wanda
E. →

90. | Vanstory, George |

A. →
   Vanover, Eva
B. →
   VanSwinderen, Floyd
C. →
   VanSyckle, Harry
D. →
   Vanture, Laurence
E. →

Questions 91-95

91. Add: 28
        +35

    A. 53   B. 62   C. 64   D. 73   E. None of these

92. Subtract: 78
             -69

    A. 7   B. 8   C. 18   D. 19   E. None of these

93. Multiply: 86
             x 6

    A. 492   B. 506   C. 516   D. 526   E. None of these

94. Divide: 8/648

    A. 71   B. 76   C. 81   D. 89   E. None of these

95. Add: 97
        +34

    A. 131   B. 132   C. 140   D. 141   E. None of these

Questions 96-100.

For Questions 96 through 100, find which one of the suggested answers appears in that question.

96. V 5 7 Z N 9 4 T

97. 4 6 P T 2 N K 9

98. 6 4 N 2 P 8 Z K

99. 7 P 5 2 4 N K T

100. K T 8 5 4 N 2 P

SUGGESTED ANSWERS
A = 2, 5, N, Z
B = 4, 5, N, P
C = 2, 9, P, T
D = 4, 9, T, Z
E = None of the above

Questions 101-105.

In Questions 101 through 105, compare the three names or numbers, and mark
- A. if ALL THREE names or numbers are exactly ALIKE
- B. if only the FIRST and SECOND names or numbers are exactly ALIKE
- C. if only the FIRST and THIRD names or numbers are exactly ALIKE
- D. if only the SECOND and THIRD names or numbers are exactly ALIKE
- E. if ALL THREE names or numbers are DIFFERENT

101. 1592514   1592574   1592574

102. 2010202   2010202   2010220

103. 6177396   6177936   6177396

104. Drusilla S. Ridgeley   Drusilla S. Ridgeley   Drusilla S. Ridgeley

105. Andrei I. Toumantzev   Andrei I. Tourmantzev   Andrei I. Toumantzov

Questions 106-110.

In Questions 106 through 110, find the correct place for the name in the box.

106. Fitzsimmons, Hugh
- A. →
  Fitts, Harold
- B. →
  Fitzgerald, June
- C. →
  FitzGibbon, Junius
- D. →
  FitzSimons, Martin
- E. →

107. D'Amato, Vincent
- A. →
  Daly, Steven
- B. →
  D'Amboise, S. Vincent
- C. →
  Daniel, Vail
- D. →
  DeAlba, Valentina
- E. →

108. | Schaeffer, Roger D. |

    A. →
       Schaffert, Evelyn M.
    B. →
       Schaffner, Margaret M.
    C. →
       Schafhirt, Milton G.
    D. →
       Shafer, Richard E.
    E. →

109. | White-Lewis, Cecil |

    A. →
       Whitelaw, Cordelia
    B. →
       White-Leigh, Nancy
    C. →
       Whitely, Rodney
    D. →
       Whitlock, Warren
    E. →

110. | VanDerHeggen, Don |

    A. →
       VanDemark, Doris
    B. →
       Vandenberg, H.E.
    C. →
       VanDercook, Marie
    D. →
       vanderLinden, Robert
    E. →

Questions 111-115.

111. Add: 75
       +49

    A. 124   B. 125   C. 134   D. 225   E. None of these

112. Subtract: 69
            - 45

    A. 14   B. 23   C. 24   D. 26   E. None of these

113. Multiply: 36
          x 8

    A. 246   B. 262   C. 288   D. 368   E. None of these

114. Divide: 8/̄3̄2̄8̄

    A. 31   B. 41   C. 42   D. 48   E. None of these

115. Multiply: 58
             x 9

    A. 472   B. 513   C. 521   D. 522   E. None of these

Questions 116-120.

For Questions 116 through 120, find which one of the suggested answers appears in that question.

116. Z 3 N P G 5 4 2

117. 6 N 2 8 G 4 P T

118. 6 N 4 T V G 8 2

119. T 3 P 4 N 8 G 2

120. 6 7 K G N 2 L 5

SUGGESTED ANSWERS:
A = 2, 3, G, N
B = 2, 6, N, T
C = 3, 4, G, K
D = 4, 6, K, T
E = None of the above

KEY (CORRECT ANSWERS)

1.	B	21	A	41.	A	61	C	81	D	101.	D
2.	E	22.	E	42.	A	62.	B	82.	C	102.	B
3.	D	23.	E	43.	B	63.	E	83.	A	103.	C
4.	A	24.	D	44.	E	64.	E	84.	D	104.	A
5.	E	25.	C	45.	A	65.	C	85.	B	105.	E
6.	E	26.	D	46.	C	66.	A	86.	A	106.	D
7.	A	27.	D	47.	A	667.	D	87.	E	107.	B
8.	D	28.	C	48.	D	68.	C	88.	C	108.	A
9.	B	29.	C	49.	B	69.	D	89.	C	109.	C
10.	E	30.	D	50.	C	70.	E	90.	B	110.	D
11.	D	31.	E	51.	B	71.	A	91.	E	111.	A
12.	B	32.	A	52.	C	72.	C	92.	E	112.	C
13.	B	33.	A	53.	D	73.	B	93.	C	113.	C
14.	B	34.	C	54.	D	74.	C	94.	C	114.	B
15.	B	35.	C	55.	E	75.	A	95.	A	115.	D
16.	A	36.	E	56.	E	76.	D	96.	D	116.	A
17.	D	37.	A	57.	B	77.	D	97.	C	117.	B
18.	E	38.	C	58.	E	78.	A	98.	E	118.	B
19.	B	39.	C	59.	D	79.	E	99.	B	119.	A
20.	A	40.	D	60.	C	80.	C	100.	B	120.	E

NAME AND NUMBER COMPARISONS

COMMENTARY

This test seeks to measure your ability and disposition to do a job carefully and accurately, your attention to exactness and preciseness of detail, your alertness and versatility in discerning similarities and differences between things, and your power in systematically handling written language symbols.

It is actually a test of your ability to do academic and/or clerical work, using the basic elements of verbal (qualitative) and mathematical (quantitative) learning—words and numbers.

EXAMINATION SECTION

TEST 1

DIRECTIONS: In each line across the page there are three names or numbers that are much alike. Compare the three names or numbers and decide which ones are exactly alike. *PRINT IN THE SPACE AT THE RIGHT THE LETTER:*
  A. if all THREE names or numbers are exactly alike
  B. if only the FIRST and SECOND names or numbers are ALIKE
  C. if only the FIRST and THIRD names or numbers are alike
  D. if only the SECOND or THIRD names or numbers are alike
  E. if ALL THREE names or numbers are DIFFERENT

1.	Davis Hazen	David Hozen	David Hazen	1.____
2.	Lois Appel	Lois Appel	Lois Apfel	2.____
3.	June Allan	Jane Allan	Jane Allan	3.____
4.	10235	10235	10235	4.____
5.	32614	32164	32614	5.____

TEST 2

1.	2395890	2395890	2395890	1.____
2.	1926341	1926347	1926314	2.____
3.	E. Owens McVey	E. Owen McVey	E. Owen McVay	3.____
4.	Emily Neal Rouse	Emily Neal Rowse	Emily Neal Rowse	4.____
5.	H. Merritt Audubon	H. Merriott Audubon	H. Merritt Audubon	5.____

TEST 3

1.	6219354	6219354	6219354	1.____
2.	231793	2312793	2312793	2.____
3.	1065407	1065407	1065047	3.____
4.	Francis Ransdell	Frances Ramsdell	Francis Ramsdell	4.____
5.	Cornelius Detwiler	Cornelius Detwiler	Cornelius Detwiler	5.____

TEST 4

1.	6452054	6452564	6542054	1.____
2.	8501268	8501268	8501286	2.____
3.	Ella Burk Newham	Ella Burk Newnham	Elena Burk Newnham	3.____
4.	Jno. K. Ravencroft	Jno. H. Ravencroft	Jno. H. Ravencoft	4.____
5.	Martin Wills Pullen	Martin Wills Pulen	Martin Wills Pullen	5.____

TEST 5

1.	3457988	3457986	3457986	1.____
2.	4695682	4695862	4695682	2.____
3.	Stricklund Kaneydy	Sticklund Kanedy	Stricklund Kanedy	3.____
4.	Joy Harlor Witner	Joy Harloe Witner	Joy Harloe Witner	4.____
5.	R.M.O. Uberroth	R.M.O. Uberroth	R.N.O. Uberroth	5.____

TEST 6

1.	1592514	1592574	1592574	1.____
2.	2010202	2010202	2010220	2.____
3.	6177396	6177936	6177396	3.____
4.	Drusilla S. Ridgeley	Drusilla S. Ridgeley	Drusilla S. Ridgeley	4.____
5.	Andrei I. Tooumantzev	Andrei I. Tourmantzev	Andrei I. Toumantzov	5.____

TEST 7

1.	5261383	5261383	5261338	1.____
2.	8125690	8126690	8125609	2.____
3.	W.E. Johnston	W.E. Johnson	W.E. Johnson	3.____
4.	Vergil L. Muller	Vergil L. Muller	Vergil L. Muller	4.____
5.	Atherton R. Warde	Asheton R. Warde	Atherton P. Warde	5.____

TEST 8

1.	013469.5	023469.5	02346.95	1.____
2.	33376	333766	333766	2.____
3.	Ling-Temco-Vought	Ling-Tenco-Vought	Ling-Temco Vought	3.____
4.	Lorilard Corp.	Lorillard Corp.	Lorrilard Corp.	4.____
5.	American Agronomics Corporation	American Agronomics Corporation	American Agronomic Corporation	5.____

4

TEST 9

1.	436592864	436592864	436592864	1.____
2.	197765123	197755123	197755123	2.____
3.	Dewaay Cortvriendt International S.A.	Deway Cortvriendt International S.A.	Deway Corturiendt International S.A.	3.____
4.	Crédit Lyonnais	Crèdit Lyonnais	Crèdit Lyonais	4.____
5.	Algemene Bank Nederland N.V.	Algamene Bank Nederland N.V.	Algemene Bank Naderland N.V.	5.____

TEST 10

1.	00032572	0.0032572	00032522	1.____
2.	399745	399745	398745	2.____
3.	Banca Privata Finanziaria S.p.A.	Banca Privata Finanzaria S.P.A.	Banca Privata Finanziaria S.P.A.	3.____
4.	Eastman Dillon, Union Securities & Co.	Eastman Dillon, Union Securities Co.	Eastman Dillon, Union Securities & Co.	4.____
5.	Arnhold and S. Bleichroeder, Inc.	Arnhold & S. Bleichroeder, Inc.	Arnold and S. Bleichroeder, Inc.	5.____

TEST 11

DIRECTIONS: Answer the questions below on the basis of the following instructions: For each such numbered set of names, addresses, and numbers listed in Columns I and II, select your answer from the following options:
- A. The names in Columns I and II are different
- B. The addresses in Columns I and II are different
- C. The numbers in Columns I and II are different
- D. The names, addresses and numbers are identical

1. Francis Jones
   62 Stately Avenue
   96-12446

   Francis Jones
   62 Stately Avenue
   96-21446

   1.____

2. Julio Montez
   19 Ponderosa Road
   56-73161

   Julio Montez
   19 Ponderosa Road
   56-71361

   2.____

3. Mary Mitchell
   2314 Melbourne Drive
   68-92172

   Mary Mitchell
   2314 Melbourne Drive
   68-92172

   3.____

4. Harry Patterson
   25 Dunne Street
   14-33430

   Harry Patterson
   25 Dunne Street
   14-34330

   4.____

5. Patrick Murphy
   171 West Hosmer Street
   93-81214

   Patrick Murphy
   171 West Hosmer Street
   93-18214

   5.____

TEST 12

1. August Schultz
816 St. Clair Avenue
53-40149

    August Schultz
816 St. Claire Avenue
53-40149

    1.____

2. George Taft
72 Runnymede Street
47-04033

    George Taft
72 Runnymede Street
47-04023

    2.____

3. Angus Henderson
1418 Madison Street
81-76375

    Angus Henderson
1418 Madison Street
81-76375

    3.____

4. Carolyn Mazur
12 Rivenlew Road
38-99615

    Carolyn Mazur
12 Rivervane Road
38-99615

    4.____

5. Adele Russell
1725 Lansing Lane
72-91962

    Adela Russell
1725 Lansing Lane
72-91962

    5.____

7

TEST 13

DIRECTIONS: The following questions are based on the instructions given below. In each of the following questions, the 3-line name and address in Column I is the master-list entry, and the 3-line entry in Column II is the information to be checked against the master list.
If there is one line that is NOT exactly alike, mark your answer A.
If there are two lines NOT exactly alike, mark your answer B.
If there are three lines NOT exactly alike, mark your answer C.
If the lines ALL are exactly alike, mark your answer D.

1. Jerome A. Jackson
   1243 14th Avenue
   New York, N.Y. 10023

   Jerome A. Johnson
   1234 14th Avenue
   New York, N.Y. 10023
   1.____

2. Sophie Strachtheim
   33-28 Connecticut Ave.
   Far Rockaway, N.Y. 11697

   Sophie Strachtheim
   33-28 Connecticut Ave.
   Far Rockaway, N.Y. 11697
   2.____

3. Elisabeth NT. Gorrell
   256 Exchange St
   New York, N.Y. 10013

   Elizabeth NT. Correll
   256 Exchange St.
   New York, N.Y. 10013
   3.____

4. Maria J. Gonzalez
   7516 E. Sheepshead Rd.
   Brooklyn, N.Y. 11240

   Maria J. Gonzalez
   7516 N. Shepshead Rd.
   Brooklyn, N.Y. 11240
   4.____

5. Leslie B. Brautenweiler
   21-57A Seller Terr.
   Flushing, N.Y. 11367

   Leslie B. Brautenwieler
   21-75ASeiler Terr.
   Flushing, N.J. 11367
   5.____

KEY (CORRECT ANSWERS)

TEST 1	TEST 2	TEST 3	TEST 4	TEST 5	TEST 6	TEST 7
1. E	1. A	1. A	1. E	1. D	1. D	1. B
2. B	2. E	2. A	2. B	2. C	2. B	2. E
3. D	3. E	3. B	3. E	3. E	3. C	3. D
4. A	4. D	4. E	4. E	4. D	4. A	4. A
5. C	5. C	5. A	5. C	5. B	5. E	5. E

TEST 8	TEST 9	TEST 10	TEST 11	TEST 12	TEST 13
1. E	1. A	1. E	1. C	1. B	1. B
2. D	2. D	2. B	2. C	2. C	2. D
3. E	3. E	3. E	3. D	3. D	3. A
4. E	4. E	4. C	4. C	4. B	4. A
5. B	5. E	5. E	5. C	5. A	5. C

NUMBER COMPARISONS
EXAMINATION SECTION
TEST 1

DIRECTIONS: This test consists of 200 questions in which pairs of numbers are to be examined for exactness. If the two numbers are exactly the same, mark the answer "A" on the line provided between the two. If they are different, mark the answer "B". This is a test for speed and accuracy. Work as fast as you can without making mistakes.

1.	307	_____	309
2.	4605	_____	4603
3.	976	_____	979
4.	101267	_____	101267
5.	3065432	_____	30965432
6.	103345700	_____	103345700
7.	46754	_____	466754
8.	3367490	_____	3367490
9.	2779	_____	2778
10.	57394	_____	57394
11.	63801829374	_____	63801839474
12.	283577657	_____	283577657
13.	75689	_____	75689
14.	2547892026	_____	2547893026
15.	336354	_____	336254
16.	998745732	_____	998745733
17.	623	_____	623
18.	263849102983	_____	263849102983
19.	5870	_____	5870
20.	379012	_____	379012
21.	8734629	_____	8734629
22.	2549806746	_____	2549806746
23.	57802564	_____	57892564
24.	689246	_____	688246
25.	1578024683	_____	1578024683
26.	582039485618	_____	582039485618
27.	63829172630	_____	63829172639
28.	592	_____	592
29.	829374820	_____	829374820
30.	62937456	_____	63937456

#	Left		Right
31.	8293	_____	8293
32.	6382910293	_____	6382910292
33.	781928374012	_____	781928374912
34.	68293	_____	38393
35.	18203649271	_____	18293649271
36.	4820384	_____	4820384
37.	283019283745	_____	283019283745
38.	73927102	_____	73927102
39.	91029354829	_____	91029354829
40.	38291728	_____	38291728
41.	6283910293	_____	6283910203
42.	392018273648	_____	392018273848
43.	820	_____	829
44.	572937273	_____	572937373
45.	7392	_____	7392
46.	8172036	_____	8172036
47.	68391028364	_____	68391028394
48.	48293	_____	48292
49.	739201	_____	739201
50.	62839201	_____	62839211
51.	5829	_____	5820
52.	192836472829	_____	192836472829
53.	362	_____	362
54.	2039271827	_____	2039276837
55.	73829	_____	73829
56.	82739102837	_____	82739102837
57.	48891028	_____	48891028
58.	7291728	_____	7291928
59.	172839102839	_____	172839102839
60.	628192	_____	628102
61.	473829432	_____	473829432
62.	478	_____	478
63.	372816253902	_____	372816252902
64.	64829	_____	64830
65.	4739210249	_____	4739210249
66.	748362	_____	748363
67.	728354792	_____	728354772
68.	3927	_____	3927
69.	927384625	_____	927384625
70.	4628156	_____	4628158

3 (#1)

#	Left		Right
71.	6382	_____	6392
72.	12937453829	_____	12937453829
73.	523	_____	533
74.	7263920	_____	7163920
75.	74293	_____	74293
76.	82734291	_____	82734271
77.	2739102637	_____	2739102637
78.	62810263849	_____	62810263846
79.	638291	_____	638291
80.	62831027	_____	62831027
81.	527	_____	529
82.	172438291026	_____	172438291026
83.	7253829142	_____	725382942
84.	836287	_____	836289
85.	62435162839	_____	62435162839
86.	6254	_____	6256
87.	6241526	_____	6241526
88.	1426389012	_____	1426389102
89.	825	_____	825
90.	67253917287	_____	67253917287
91.	6271	_____	6271
92.	263819253627	_____	263819253629
93.	82637	_____	82937
94.	728392736	_____	728392736
95.	62739	_____	32739
96.	728352689	_____	728352688
97.	463728	_____	463728
98.	73829176	_____	73827196
99.	4825367	_____	4825369
100.	56382018	_____	56382018
101.	789	_____	789
102.	819263728192	_____	819263728172
103.	682537289	_____	682537298
104.	7245	_____	7245
105.	82936542891	_____	82936542891
106.	4738267	_____	4737277
107.	63728	_____	63729
108.	6283628901	_____	6283628991
109.	918264	_____	918264
110.	263728192037	_____	263728192073

4 (#1)

111.	528391025283910238	_____	52839102738
112.	6283	_____	6182
113.	7283529152	_____	7283529152
114.	208	_____	298
115.	82637201927	_____	8263720127
116.	15273826	_____	15273826
117.	72537	_____	73537
118.	726391027384	_____	726391027384
119.	627389	_____	627399
120.	7253829910	_____	725382910
121.	46273	_____	46273
122.	629	_____	620
123.	7382517283	_____	7382517283
124.	637281	_____	528281
125.	2738261	_____	2728261
126.	627152637490	_____	627152637490
127.	73526189	_____	73526189
128.	5372	_____	5392
129.	63728142	_____	63728142
130.	4783946	_____	4783046
131.	826372810428	_____	82637281028
132.	628	_____	628
133.	7293728172	_____	7293728177
134.	7362	_____	7362
135.	927382615	_____	927382615
136.	84345	_____	85345
137.	894643278	_____	895642377
138.	726352	_____	726353
139.	7263524	_____	7263524
140.	632685	_____	632685
141.	273648293048	_____	273648293048
142.	634	_____	634
143.	7362536478	_____	7362536478
144.	7362	_____	7363
145.	7362819273	_____	7362819273
146.	63728	_____	63738
147	63728192637	_____	63728192639
148.	728	_____	738
149.	62738291527	_____	62738291529
150.	63728192	_____	63728192

5 (#1)

#	Left	Right
151.	73526	73525
152.	728367189	7283627189
153.	627	637
154.	728352617283	7283526617282
155.	6281	6381
156.	936271826	936371826
157.	82637192037	72636192936
158.	527182	527182
159.	6273	6273
160.	726354256	72635456
161.	725361552637	725361555637
162.	7526378	7526377
163.	685	685
164.	82637481028	82637481028
165.	3427	3429
166.	82736493351	82736493351
167.	63728	63728
168.	6273846273	6273846293
169.	62836	6283
170.	2638496	2637496
171.	738291627874	738291627874
172.	62826454	62836455
173.	42738267	42738269
174.	573929	573829
175.	628364728	628364928
176.	725	735
177.	627385	627383
178.	63354	63354
179	54283902	54283602
180	7283562781	7283562781
181.	62738	63738
182.	72735542321	72735542321
183.	263849332	263849332
184.	162837	163837
185.	47382912	47382922

6 (#1)

#	Left		Right
186.	628367299	_____	628367399
187.	111	_____	111
188.	11829304829	_____	11828304829
189.	4448	_____	4448
190.	333693678	_____	333693678
191.	3212	_____	3212
192.	27389223678	_____	27389223678
193.	473829	_____	473829
194.	7382937	_____	7383937
195.	3628901223	_____	3628901233
196.	5572867	_____	5572867
197.	87263543	_____	87263543
198.	3678902	_____	3678892
199.	15672839	_____	15672839
200.	9927382	_____	9927382

KEY (CORRECT ANSWERS)

1.	B	41.	B	81.	B	121.	A	161.	B
2.	B	42.	B	82.	A	122.	B	162.	B
3.	B	43.	B	83.	B	123.	A	163.	A
4.	A	44.	B	84.	B	124.	B	164.	A
5.	B	45.	A	85.	A	125.	B	165.	B
6.	A	46.	A	86.	B	126.	A	166.	B
7.	B	47.	B	87.	A	127.	A	167.	A
8.	A	48.	B	88.	B	128.	B	168.	B
9.	B	49.	A	89.	A	129.	B	169.	B
10.	A	50.	B	90.	A	130.	B	170.	A
11.	B	51.	B	91.	A	131.	A	171.	A
12.	A	52.	A	92.	B	132.	A	172.	B
13.	A	53.	A	93.	B	133.	B	173.	B
14.	B	54.	B	94.	A	134.	A	174.	A
15.	B	55.	A	95.	A	135.	A	175.	B
16.	B	56.	A	96.	B	136.	A	176.	B
17.	A	57.	A	97.	A	137.	B	177.	B
18.	A	58.	B	98.	B	138.	B	178.	A
19.	A	59.	A	99.	B	139.	A	179.	B
20.	A	60.	B	100.	A	140.	A	180.	A
21.	A	61.	A	101.	A	141.	A	181.	B
22.	A	62.	A	102.	B	142.	A	182.	B
23.	B	63.	A	103.	B	143.	A	183.	A
24.	B	64.	B	104.	A	144.	B	184.	B
25.	A	65.	A	105.	A	145.	A	185.	B
26.	A	66.	B	106.	B	146.	B	186.	B
27.	B	67.	B	107.	B	147.	B	187.	A
28.	A	68.	A	108.	B	148.	B	188.	B
29.	A	69.	A	109.	A	149.	B	189.	A
30.	B	70.	B	110.	B	150.	B	190.	A
31.	A	71.	B	111.	B	151.	A	191.	A
32.	B	72.	A	112.	B	152.	A	192.	A
33.	B	73.	B	113.	A	153.	B	193.	A
34.	B	74.	A	114.	B	154.	B	194.	B
35.	B	75.	A	115.	B	155.	B	195.	B
36.	A	76.	B	116.	A	156.	A	196.	A
37.	A	77.	A	117.	B	157.	A	197.	A
38.	A	78.	B	118.	A	158.	A	198.	B
39.	A	79.	A	119.	B	159.	A	199.	A
40.	A	80.	A	120.	A	160.	B	200.	A

NAME AND NUMBER CHECKING
EXAMINATION SECTION
TEST 1

DIRECTIONS: This test is designed to measure your speed/and accuracy. You are urged to work both quickly and accurately and to do correctly as many lists as you can in the time allowed. The test consists of lists or pairs of names and numbers. Count the number of IDENTICAL pairs in each list. Then, select the correct number, 1, 2, 3, 4, 5, and indicate your choice in the space at the right. Two sample questions are presented for your guidance, together with the correct solutions.

<u>SAMPLE LIST A</u>
Adelphi College – Adelphia College
Braxton Corp – Braxeton Corp.
Wassaic State School – Wassaic State School
Central Islip State Hospital – Central Isllip State Hospital
Greenwich House – Greenwich House

NOTE: There are only two correct pairs—Wassaic State School and Greenwich House. Therefore, the CORRECT answer is 2.

<u>SAMPLE LIST B</u>
78453694 – 78453684
784530 – 784530
533 – 534
67845 – 67845
2368745 – 2368755

NOTE: There are only two correct pairs—784530 and 67845. Therefore, the CORRECT answer is 2.

<u>LIST 1</u>   1.____
    Diagnostic Clinic   – Diagnostic Clinic
    Yorkville Health   – Yorkville Health
    Meinhard Clinic   – Meinhart Clinic
    Corlears Clinic   – Carlears Clinic
    Tremont Diagnostic – Tremont Diagnostic

<u>LIST 2</u>   2.____
    73526   – 73526
    7283627198   – 7283627198
    627   – 637
    728352617283 – 7283526178282
    6281   – 6281

2 (#1)

LIST 3   3.____
    Jefferson Clinic   – Jeffersen Clinic
    Mott Haven Center   – Mott Havan Center
    Bronx Hospital   – Bronx Hospital
    Montefiore Hospital   – Montifeore Hospital
    Beth Isreal Hospital   – Beth Israel Hospital

LIST 4   4.____
    936271826   – 936371826
    5271   – 5291
    82637192037   – 82637192037
    527182   – 5271882
    726354256   - 72635456

LIST 5   5.____
    Trinity Hospital   – Trinity Hospital
    Central Harlem   – Centrel Harlem
    St. Luke's Hospital   – St. Lukes' Hospital
    Mt. Sinai Hospital   – Mt. Sinia Hospital
    N.Y. Dispensery   – N.Y. Dispensary

LIST 6   6.____
    725361552637   – 725361555637
    7526378   – 7526377
    6975   – 6975
    82637481028   – 82637481028
    3427   – 3429

LIST 7   7.____
    Misericordia Hospital   – Miseracordia Hospital
    Lebonan Hospital   – Lebanon Hospital
    Gouverneur Hospital   – Gouverner Hospital
    German Polyclinic   – German Policlinic
    French Hospital   – French Hospital

LIST 8   8.____
    8277364933251   – 827364933351
    63728   – 63728
    367281   – 367281
    62733846273   – 6273846293
    62836   - 6283

LIST 9   9.____
    King's County Hospital   – Kings County Hospital
    St. Johns Long Island   – St. John's Long Island
    Bellevue Hospital   – Bellvue Hospital
    Beth David Hospital   – Beth David Hospital
    Samaritan Hospital   – Samariton Hospital

3 (#1)

LIST 10   10.____
   62836454   – 62836455
   42738267   – 42738369
   573829   – 573829
   738291627874   – 738291627874
   725   - 735

LIST 11   11.____
   Bloomingdal Clinic   – Bloomingdale Clinic
   Communitty Hospital   – Community Hospital
   Metroplitan Hospital – Metropoliton Hospital
   Lenox Hill Hospital   – Lonex Hill Hospital
   Lincoln Hospital   – Lincoln Hospital

LIST 12   12.____
   6283364728   – 6283648
   627385   – 627383
   54283902   – 54283602
   63354   – 63354
   7283562781   - 7283562781

LIST 13   13.____
   Sydenham Hospital   – Sydanham Hospital
   Roosevalt Hospital   – Roosevelt Hospital
   Vanderbilt Clinic   – Vanderbild Clinic
   Women's Hospital   – Woman's Hospital
   Flushing Hospital   – Flushing Hospital

LIST 14   14.____
   62738   – 62738
   727355542321   – 72735542321
   263849332   – 263849332
   262837   – 263837
   47382912   - 47382922

LIST 15   15.____
   Episcopal Hospital   – Episcapal Hospital
   Flower Hospital   – Flouer Hospital
   Stuyvesent Clinic   – Stuyvesant Clinic
   Jamaica Clinic   – Jamaica Clinic
   Ridgwood Clinic   – Ridgewood Clinic

LIST 16   16.____
   628367299   – 628367399
   111   – 111
   118293304829   – 1182839489
   4448   – 4448
   333693678   - 333693678

4 (#1)

LIST 17   17.____
    Arietta Crane Farm   – Areitta Crane Farm
    Bikur Chilim Home   – Bikur Chilom Home
    Burke Foundation   – Burke Foundation
    Blythedale Home   – Blythdale Home
    Campbell Cottages   – Cambell Cottages

LIST 18   18.____
    32123   – 32132
    273893326783   – 27389326783
    473829   – 473829
    7382937   – 7383937
    3628890122332   - 36289012332

LIST 19   19.____
    Caraline Rest   – Caroline Rest
    Loreto Rest   – Loretto Rest
    Edgewater Creche   – Edgwater Creche
    Holiday Farm   – Holiday Farm
    House of St. Giles   – House of st. Giles

LIST 20   20.____
    557286777   – 55728677
    3678902   – 3678892
    1567839   – 1567839
    7865434712   – 7865344712
    9927382   - 9927382

LIST 21   21.____
    Isabella Home   – Isabela Home
    James A. Moore Home   – James A. More Home
    The Robin's Nest   – The Roben's Nest
    Pelham Home   – Pelam Home
    St. Eleanora's Home   – St. Eleanora's Home

LIST 22   22.____
    273648293048   – 273648293048
    334   – 334
    7362536478   – 7362536478
    7362819273   – 7362819273
    7362   - 7363

LIST 23   23.____
    St. Pheobe's Mission   – St. Phebe's Mission
    Seaside Home   – Seaside Home
    Speedwell Society   – Speedwell Society
    Valeria Home   – Valera Home
    Wiltwyck   - Wildwyck

5 (#1)

LIST 24
    63728   – 63738
    63728192736   – 63728192738
    428   – 458
    62738291527   – 62738291529
    63728192   - 63728192

24.____

LIST 25
    McGaffin   – McGafin
    David Ardslee   – David Ardslee
    Axton Supply   – Axeton Supply Co
    Alice Russell   – Alice Russell
    Dobson Mfg. Co. – Dobsen Mfg. Co.

25.____

KEY (CORRECT ANSWERS)

1.	3		11.	1
2.	3		12.	2
3.	1		13.	1
4.	1		14.	2
5.	1		15.	1
6.	2		16.	3
7.	1		17.	1
8.	2		18.	1
9.	1		19.	1
10.	2		20.	2

21.	1
22.	4
23.	2
24.	1
25.	2

TEST 2

DIRECTIONS: This test is designed to measure your speed/and accuracy. You are urged to work both quickly and accurately and to do correctly as many lists as you can in the time allowed. The test consists of lists or pairs of names and numbers. Count the number of IDENTICAL pairs in each list. Then, select the correct number, 1, 2, 3, 4, 5, and indicate your choice in the space at the right.

LIST 1
    82637381028   – 82637281028
    928   – 928
    72937281028   – 72937281028
    7362   – 7362
    927382615   – 927382615

1.____

LIST 2
    Albee Theatre   – Albee Theatre
    Lapland Lumber Co.   – Laplund Lumber Co.
    Adelphi College   – Adelphi College
    Jones & Son Inc.   – Jones & Sons Inc.
    S.W. Ponds Co.   – S.W. Ponds Co.

2.____

LIST 3
    85345   – 85345
    895643278   – 895643277
    726352   – 726353
    632685   – 632685
    7263524   – 7236524

3.____

LIST 4
    Eagle Library   – Eagle Library
    Dodge Ltd.   – Dodge Co.
    Stromberg Carlson   – Stromberg Carlsen
    Clairice Ling   – Clairice Linng
    Mason Book Co.   – Matson Book Co.

4.____

LIST 5
    66273   – 66273
    629   – 629
    7382517283   – 7382517283
    637281   – 639281
    2738261   – 2788261

5.____

LIST 6
    Robert MacColl   – Robert McColl
    Buick Motor   – Buck Motors
    Murray Bay & Co. Ltd.   – Murray Bay Co. Ltd.
    L.T. Ltyle   – L.T. Lyttle
    A.S. Landas   – A.S. Landas

6.____

LIST 7
    6271526374890   – 627152637490
    73526189   – 73526189
    5372   – 5392
    637281142   – 63728124
    4783946   – 4783046

7.____

LIST 8
    Tyndall Burke   – Tyndell Burke
    W. Briehl   – W. Briehl
    Burritt Publishing Co.   – Buritt Publishing Co.
    Frederick Breyer & Co.   – Frederick Breyer Co.
    Bailey Buulard   – Bailey Bullard

8.____

LIST 9
    634   – 634
    16837   – 163837
    273892223678   – 27389223678
    527182   – 527782
    3628901223   – 3629002223

9.____

LIST 10
    Ernest Boas   – Ernest Boas
    Rankin Barne   – Rankin Barnes
    Edward Appley   – Edward Appely
    Camel   – Camel
    Caiger Food Co.   – Caiger Food Co.

10.____

LIST 11
    6273   – 6273
    322   – 332
    15672839   – 15672839
    63728192637   – 63728192639
    738   – 738

11.____

LIST 12
    Wells Fargo Co.   – Wells Fargo Co.
    W.D. Brett   – W.D. Britt
    Tassco Co.   – Tassko Co
    Republic Mills   – Republic Mill
    R.W. Burnham   – R.W. Burhnam

12.____

LIST 13
    7253529152   – 7283529152
    6283   – 6383
    52839102738   – 5283910238
    308   – 398
    82637201927   – 8263720127

13.____

3 (#2)

LIST 14   14.____
    Schumacker Co.   – Shumacker Co.
    C.H. Caiger   – C.H. Caiger
    Abraham Strauss   – Abram Straus
    B.F. Boettjer   – B.F. Boettijer
    Cut-Rate Store   – Cut-Rate Stores

LIST 15   15.____
    15273826   – 15273826
    72537   – 73537
    726391027384   – 62639107384
    637389   – 627399
    725382910   – 725382910

LIST 16   16.____
    Hixby Ltd.   – Hixby Lt'd.
    S. Reiner   – S. Riener
    Reynard Co.   – Reynord Co.
    Esso Gassoline Co.   – Esso Gasolene Co.
    Belle Brock   – Belle Brock

LIST 17   17.____
    7245   – 7245
    819263728192   – 819263728172
    682537289   – 682537298
    789   – 789
    82936542891   – 82936542891

LIST 18   18.____
    Joseph Cartwright   – Joseph Cartwrite
    Foote Food Co.   – Foot Food Co.
    Weiman & Held   – Weiman & Held
    Sanderson Shoe Co.   – Sandersen Shoe Co.
    A.M. Byrne   – A.N. Byrne

LIST 19   19.____
    4738267   – 4738277
    63728   – 63729
    6283628901   – 6283628991
    918264   – 918264
    263728192037   – 2637728192073

LIST 20   20.____
    Exray Laboratories   – Exray Labratories
    Curley Toy Co.   – Curly Toy Co.
    J. Lauer & Cross   – J. Laeur & Cross
    Mireco Brands   – Mireco Brands
    Sandor Lorand   – Sandor Larand

4 (#2)

LIST 21   21.____
    607   – 609
    6405   – 6403
    976   – 996
    101267   – 101267
    2065432   – 20965432

LIST 22   22.____
    John Macy & Sons   – John Macy & Son
    Venus Pencil Co.   – Venus Pencil Co.
    Nell McGinnis   – Nell McGinnis
    McCutcheon & Co.   – McCutcheon & Co.
    Sun-Tan Oil   – Sun-Tan Oil

LIST 23   23.____
    703345700   – 703345700
    46754   – 466754
    3367490   – 3367490
    3379   – 3778
    47384   – 47394

LIST 24   24.____
    arthritis   – arthritis
    asthma   – asthma
    endocrine   – endocrene
    gastro-enterological – gastrol-enteralogical
    orthopedic   – orthopedic

LIST 25   25.____
    743829432   – 743828432
    998   – 998
    732816253902 – 732816252902
    46829   – 46830
    7439120249   – 7439210249

KEY (CORRECT ANSWERS)

1.	4	11.	3
2.	3	12.	1
3.	2	13.	1
4.	1	14.	1
5.	2	15.	2
6.	1	16.	1
7.	2	17.	3
8.	1	18.	1
9.	1	19.	1
10.	3	20.	1

21. 1
22. 4
23. 2
24. 3
25. 1

ARITHMETIC

EXAMINATION SECTION
TEST 1

DIRECTIONS: Each question or incomplete statement is followed by several suggested answers or completions. Select the one that BEST answers the question or completes the statement. *PRINT THE LETTER OF THE CORRECT ANSWER IN THE SPACE AT THE RIGHT.*

1. 215 x 30 =

    A. 650
    B. 6450
    C. 6500
    D. None of the above

    1.____

2. How much is saved by buying a $60 bicycle for cash instead of paying $5.25 a month for a year?

    A. $3.00
    B. $6.00
    C. $7.50
    D. None of the above

    2.____

3. How many square inches are in a square foot?

    A. 12
    B. 24
    C. 144
    D. None of the above

    3.____

4. What is ten thousand multiplied by one thousand?

    A. One hundred thousand
    B. One million
    C. Ten million
    D. None of the above

    4.____

5. $4 \frac{1}{6} + 3 \frac{1}{12} =$

    A. $7 \frac{1}{4}$
    B. $7 \frac{7}{12}$
    C. $8 \frac{1}{4}$
    D. None of the above

    5.____

6. Tom is awake an average of 15 hours each day. How many hours does he sleep in a week?

    A. 9
    B. 45
    C. 105
    D. None of the above

    6.____

7. If peppermints costing 70¢ per lb. come in 1 1/2 lb. boxes, what is the cost of 5 boxes?

    A. $3.50
    B. $5.25
    C. $5.75
    D. None of the above

    7.____

8. What is 349,638 rounded to the nearest hundred?

    A. 349,600
    B. 349,640
    C. 350,000
    D. None of the above

    8.____

9. 6 1/9 - 3 1/3 =

   A. 2 7/9
   B. 2 8/9
   C. 3 1/2
   D. None of the above

10. Which is less than one-thousandth of an inch?

    A. .025 in.
    B. .004 in.
    C. .0008 in.
    D. None of the above

11. Which is ten million three thousand?

    A. 10,300,000
    B. 10,030,000
    C. 10,003,000
    D. None of the above

12. $\frac{1}{2} + \frac{1}{3} + \frac{1}{6}$

    A. $\frac{1}{11}$
    B. $\frac{5}{6}$
    C. 1
    D. None of the above

13. 2/5 of 20 =

    A. 1/8
    B. 8
    C. 50
    D. None of the above

14. In the following multiplication, N stands for a number.

    4N5
       4
    ―――
    1740

    What is the number?

    A. 3
    B. 6
    C. 8
    D. None of the above

15. 7/8 - 1/2

    A. 3/8
    B. 3/4
    C. 1
    D. None of the above

16. The scale for a house plan is 1/4 in. =1 ft.
    How long is a hall that is 3 inches long on the plan?

    A. 7 ft.
    B. $12\frac{1}{2}$ ft.
    C. 16 ft.
    D. None of the above

17. 4 1/5 x 1 3/7 =

    A. 5
    B. 5 22/35
    C. 6
    D. None of the above

18. 7/3 - 11/6

    A. 1/2
    B. 1 3/11
    C. 1 1/3
    D. None of the above

19. The school pool is 60 feet long.
    How many lengths must John swim to pass his 100-yard swimming test?

    A. 2
    B. 5
    C. 6
    D. None of the above

20. A store bought a dozen clocks for $72 and sold each for 50% more than it cost. What was the selling price of one clock?

    A. $6.50
    B. $9.00
    C. $26.00
    D. None of the above

21. If J stands for John's age and F for his father's age, which shows that John is 26 years younger than his father?

    A. J + F = 26
    B. J - 26 = F
    C. J + 26 = F
    D. None of the above

22. The board at the right has five equally spaced holes. What is the distance between the centers of holes 2 and 3?

    A. 8"
    B. 10"
    C. 20"
    D. None of the above

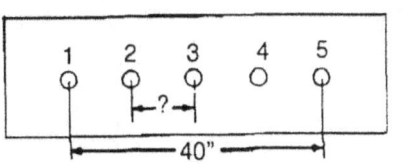

23. $.07 \overline{) 51.1} =$

    A. 7.3
    B. 73
    C. 730
    D. None of the above

24. Joe worked from 8:30 A.M. until 4:45 P.M., except for 45 minutes for lunch. How many hours did he work?

    A. $6\frac{1}{2}$
    B. $7\frac{1}{2}$
    C. $8\frac{1}{2}$
    D. None of the above

25. A highway 150 miles long cost $130 million. What was the AVERAGE cost per mile?

    A. Between $12,000 and $13,000
    B. Between $200,000 and $300,000
    C. Between $800,000 and $900,000
    D. None of the above

KEY (CORRECT ANSWERS)

1. B
2. A
3. C
4. C
5. A

6. D
7. B
8. A
9. A
10. C

11. C
12. C
13. B
14. A
15. A

16. D
17. C
18. A
19. B
20. B

21. C
22. B
23. C
24. B
25. C

SOLUTIONS TO PROBLEMS

1. $(215)(30) = 6450$

2. Savings $= (\$5.25)(12) - \$60 = \$3.00$

3. $(12)(12) = 144$ sq.in. $= 1$ sq.ft.

4. $(10,000)(1000) = 10,000,000 =$ ten million

5. $4\frac{1}{6} + 3\frac{1}{12} = 4\frac{2}{12} + 3\frac{1}{12} = 7\frac{3}{12} = 7\frac{1}{4}$

6. $(9)(7) = 63$ hours of sleep per week

7. $(5)(1\frac{1}{2})(.70) = \$5.25$

8. $349,638 = 349,600$ when rounded to the nearest hundred

9. $6\frac{1}{9} - 3\frac{1}{3} = 6\frac{1}{9} - 3\frac{3}{9} = 5\frac{10}{9} - 3\frac{3}{9} = 2\frac{7}{9}$

10. .0008 in. is less than .001 in.

11. $10,003,000 =$ ten million three thousand

12. $\frac{1}{2} + \frac{1}{3} + \frac{1}{6} = \frac{3}{6} + \frac{2}{6} + \frac{1}{6} = 1$

13. $(\frac{2}{5})(\frac{20}{1}) = \frac{40}{5} = 8$

14. If $N = 3$, we have $(435)(4) = 1740$. Note: $(5)(4) = 0$ digit and a carry-over of 2 in this multiplication. So, $4 \times N + 2 = 1$ digit Only $N = 3$ or $N = 8$ would fit. But note that the final answer of 1740 would eliminate 8 as a choice.

15. $\frac{7}{8} - \frac{1}{2} = \frac{7}{8} - \frac{4}{8} = \frac{3}{8}$

16. $3" \div \frac{1}{4} = 12$. Then, $(12)(1 \text{ ft.}) = 12$ ft.

17. $4\frac{1}{5} \times 1\frac{3}{7} = (\frac{21}{5})(\frac{10}{7}) = \frac{210}{35} = 6$

18. $\frac{7}{3} - \frac{11}{6} = \frac{14}{6} - \frac{11}{6} = \frac{3}{6} = \frac{1}{2}$

19. 100 yds. = 300 ft. Then, 300 ÷ 60 = 5 lengths

20. $72 12 = $6.00. Then, ($6.00)(1.50) = $9.00

21. J + 26 = F shows that John is 26 years younger than his father.

22. The distance from hole 1 to hole 5 = 40", so the distance between any two consecutive holes = 40" ÷ 4 = 10"

23. 51.1 ÷ .07 = 730

24. From 8:30 AM to 4:45 PM = 8 8i hrs. Then, hrs. of 3 work. (Note: 45 min. = 3/4 hr.)

25. $130,000,000 ÷ 150 = = $866,666.67 average cost per mile.

   This figure is between $800,000 and $900,000.

TEST 2

DIRECTIONS: Each question or incomplete statement is followed by several suggested answers or completions. Select the one that BEST answers the question or completes the statement. *PRINT THE LETTER OF THE CORRECT ANSWER IN THE SPACE AT THE RIGHT.*

1. What is the volume of the box shown at the right?
   A. 7 cu. ft.
   B. 12 cu. ft.
   C. 14 cu. ft.
   D. None of the above

   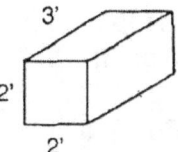

   1._____

2. If lemonade is made by mixing 1 pint of lemon juice with 3 quarts of water, how much lemon juice should be mixed with 3 gallons of water?

   A. 2 quarts
   B. 3 quarts
   C. 1 gallon
   D. None of the above

   2._____

3. What is the area of the figure shown at the right?
   A. 3 sq. in.
   B. 5 sq. in.
   C. 10 sq. in.
   D. None of the above

   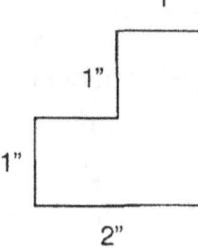

   3._____

4. $\dfrac{21 \times 14 \times 30}{28 \times 15 \times 7} =$

   A. 2
   B. 3
   C. 21
   D. None of the above

   4._____

5. 125% of 60 =

   A. 75
   B. 750
   C. 7500
   D. None of the above

   5._____

6. In the formula I = .05pt, I is the interest due on p dollars borrowed at 5% for t years. What is I if p = $500?

   A. 25t
   B. .10t
   C. .05(500+t)
   D. None of the above

   6._____

7. 4 x 6 = ? x 8. ? =

   A. 3
   B. 24
   C. 192
   D. None of the above

   7._____

8. On a day in January, the temperature in Central City was -18° F. How many degrees below freezing was this?

   A. 14
   B. 18
   C. 50
   D. None of the above

   8._____

9. .875 =

   A. $\dfrac{875}{100}$
   B. $\dfrac{5}{8}$
   C. 7 / 2
   D. None of the above

10. What is the area of the right triangle shown at the right?
    A. 6 sq. ft.
    B. 12 sq. ft.
    C. 60 sq. ft.
    D. None of the above

11. A United States Savings Bond costs $18.75. How many can be bought for $150?

    A. 6
    B. 8
    C. 12
    D. None of the above

12. One half of a melon was divided equally among 4 boys. What portion of the whole melon did each boy get?

    A. 1/8
    B. 1/6
    C. 1/4
    D. None of the above

13. One third of a foot is what part of a yard?

    A. 1/6
    B. 1/9
    C. 1/12
    D. None of the above

14. What is the sum of XXVIII and XII?

    A. D
    B. XC
    C. XL
    D. None of the above

15. How many people can each have pint of punch from one gallon of punch?

    A. 8
    B. 16
    C. 32
    D. None of the above

16. How much are license plates for a car weighing 3500 lbs. if the cost is $.50 per 100 lbs.?

    A. $17.50
    B. $35.00
    C. $70.00
    D. None of the above

17. What percent of the figure is black?

    A. 20%
    B. 25%
    C. 33 1/3%
    D. None of the above

18. Each week, Bill saves $2 of his own money and $3 given him by his father. When the total is $25, how much of it was from Bill's own money?

    A. $10.00
    B. $12.50
    C. $20.00
    D. None of the above

19. $\dfrac{3}{8} \div \dfrac{1}{4}$

    A. 25   B. .5
    C. 1.5   D. None of the above

19.____

20. If the price of a $5 tablecloth is reduced by $1, what is the percent reduction?

    A. 4%   B. 20%
    C. 25%   D. None of the above

20.____

KEY (CORRECT ANSWERS)

1.	B	11.	B
2.	A	12.	A
3.	A	13.	B
4.	B	14.	C
5.	A	15.	B
6.	A	16.	A
7.	A	17.	B
8.	C	18.	A
9.	C	19.	C
10.	A	20.	B

4 (#2)

SOLUTIONS TO PROBLEMS

1. Volume = (2')(2')(3') = 12 cu.ft.

2. 3 gallons = 12 qts. and 12 qts. 3 qts. = 4.
   Thus, (1 pt)(4) = 4 pts = 2 qts of lemon juice.

3. Area of I = 1" x 1" = 1 sq.in.
   Area of II = 2" x 1" = 2 sq.in.
   Total area = 3 sq.in.

4. $[(21)(14)(30)] \div [(28)(15)(7)] = 8820 \div 2940 = 3$

5. (1.25)(60) = 75

6. I = (.05)($500)(t) = 25t

7. 4 x 6 = 24. Then, 24 ÷ 8 = 3

8. -18°F = 32° - (-18°) = 50° below freezing

9. $.875 = \dfrac{875}{1000} = \dfrac{7}{8}$

10. Area = (1/2)(3')(4') = 6 sq.ft.

11. $150 ÷ $18.75 = 8 bonds

12. $\dfrac{1}{2} \div 4 = \dfrac{1}{2} \times \dfrac{1}{4} = \dfrac{1}{8}$ melon

13. $\dfrac{1}{3}$ ft = $(\dfrac{1}{3})(12") = 4"$ and $\dfrac{4"}{36"} = \dfrac{1}{9}$ yd.

14. XXVIII + XII = 28 + 12 = 40 = XL

15. 1 gallon = 8 pints. 8 Pints ÷ $\dfrac{1}{2}$ Pint = 16 servings

16. 3500 ÷ 100 = 35, so (35)($.50) = $17.50

17. $\dfrac{3}{12}$ = 25% of these boxes are black

18. Let x = Bill's own money. Then, $\dfrac{2}{5} = \dfrac{x}{25}$ Solving, x = $10

19. $\dfrac{3}{8} \div \dfrac{1}{4} = \left(\dfrac{3}{8}\right)\left(\dfrac{4}{1}\right) = \dfrac{12}{8} = 1.5$

20. $\dfrac{1}{5}$ = 20% reduction

ARITHMETICAL COMPUTATION AND REASONING
EXAMINATION SECTION
TEST 1

DIRECTIONS: Each question or incomplete statement is followed by several suggested answers or completions. Select the one that BEST answers the question or completes the statement. *PRINT THE LETTER OF THE CORRECT ANSWER IN THE SPACE AT THE RIGHT.*

1. 3/8 less than $40 is

   A. $25   B. $65   C. $15   D. $55

   1._____

2. 27/64 expressed as a percent is

   A. 40.625%   B. 42.188%   C. 43.750%   D. 45.313%

   2._____

3. 1/6 more than 36 gross is _____ gross.

   A. 6   B. 48   C. 30   D. 42

   3._____

4. 15 is 20% of

   4._____

5. The number which when increased by 1/3 of itself equals 96 is

   A. 128   B. 72   C. 64   D. 32

   5._____

6. 0.16 3/4 written as percent is

   A. 16 3/4%   B. 16.3/4%   C. .016 3/4%   D. .0016 3/4%

   6._____

7. 55% of 15 is

   A. 82.5   B. 0.825   C. 0.0825   D. 8.25

   7._____

8. The number which when decreased by 1/3 of itself equals 96 is

   A. 64   B. 32   C. 128   D. 144

   8._____

9. A carpenter used a board 15 3/4 ft. long from which 3 footstools were made with sufficient lumber left over for half of another footstool.
   If the lumber cost 24 1/2¢ per foot, the cost of EACH footstool was

   A. $1.54   B. $3.86   C. $1.10   D. $1.08

   9._____

10. In one year, a luncheonette purchased 1231 gallons of milk for $907.99.
    The AVERAGE cost per half pint was

    A. $0.046   B. $0.045   C. $0.047   D. $0.044

    10._____

11. The product of 23 and 9 3/4 is

    A. 191 2/3   B. 224 1/4   C. 213 3/4   D. 32 3/4

    11._____

12. An order for 345 machine bolts at $4.15 per hundred will cost

    A. $0.1432   B. $1.1432   C. $14.32   D. $143.20

    12._____

13. The fractional equivalent of .0625 is

    A. 1/16   B. 1/15   C. 1/14   D. 1/13

14. The number 0.03125 equals

    A. 3/64   B. 1/16   C. 1/64   D. 1/32

15. 21.70 divided by 1.75 equals

    A. 124   B. 12.4   C. 1.24   D. .124

16. The average cost of school lunches for 100 children varied as follows: Monday, $0.285; Tuesday, $0.237; Wednesday, $0.264; Thursday, $0.276; Friday, $0.292. The AVERAGE lunch cost

    A. $0.136   B. $0.270   C. $0.135   D. $0.271

17. The cost of 5 dozen eggs at $8.52 per gross is

    A. $3.50   B. $42.60   C. $3.55   D. $3.74

18. 410.07 less 38.49 equals

    A. 372.58   B. 371.58   C. 381.58   D. 382.68

19. The cost of 7 3/4 tons of coal at $20.16 per ton is

    A. $15.12   B. $151.20   C. $141.12   D. $156.24

20. The sum of 90.79, 79.09, 97.90, and 9.97 is

    A. 277.75   B. 278.56   C. 276.94   D. 277.93

KEY (CORRECT ANSWERS)

1.	A	11.	B
2.	B	12.	C
3.	D	13.	A
4.	C	14.	D
5.	B	15.	B
6.	A	16.	D
7.	D	17.	C
8.	D	18.	B
9.	C	19.	D
10.	A	20.	A

3 (#1)

SOLUTIONS TO PROBLEMS

1. ($40)(5/8) = $25

2. 27/64 = .421875 ≈ 42.188%

3. (36)(1 1/6) = 42

4. Let x = missing number. Then, 15 = .20x. Solving, x = 75

5. Let x = missing number. Then, x + 1/3 x = 96. Simplifying, 4/3 x = 96. Solving, x = 96 ÷ 4/3 = 72

6. .16 3/4 = 16 3/4% by simply moving the decimal point two places to the right.

7. (.55)(15) = 8.25

8. Let x = missing number. Then, x - 1/3 x = 96. Simplifying, 2/3 x = 96. Solving, x = 96 ÷ 2/3 = 144

9. 15 3/4 ÷ 3 1/2 = 4.5 feet per footstool. The cost of one footstool is ($.245)(4.5) = $1.1025 ≈ $1.10

10. $907.99 ÷ 1231 = $.7376 per gallon. Since there are 16 half-pints in a gallon, the average cost per half-pint is $.7376 ÷ 16 ≈ $.046

11. (23)(9 3/4) = (23)(9.75) = 224.25 or 224 1/4

12. ($4.15)(3.45) = $14.3175 = $14.32

13. .0625 = 625/10,000 = 1/16

14. .03125 = 3125/100,000 = 1/32

15. 21.70 ÷ 1.75 = 12.4

16. The sum of these lunches is $1.354. Then, $1.354 ÷ 5 = $.2708 = $.271

17. $8.52 ÷ 12 = $.71 per dozen. Then, the cost of 5 dozen is ($.71)(5) = $3.55

18. 410.07 - 38.49 = 371.58

19. ($20.16)(7.75) = $156.24

20. 90.79 + 79.09 + 97.90 + 9.97 = 277.75

TEST 2

DIRECTIONS: Each question or incomplete statement is followed by several suggested answers or completions. Select the one that BEST answers the question or completes the statement. *PRINT THE LETTER OF THE CORRECT ANSWER IN THE SPACE AT THE RIGHT.*

1. 1600 is 40% of what number?
   A. 6400　　B. 3200　　C. 4000　　D. 5600

2. An executive's time card reads: Arrived 9:15 A.M., Left 2:05 P.M. How many hours was he in the office? _____ hours _____ minutes.
   A. 5; 10　　B. 4; 50　　C. 4; 10　　D. 5; 50

3. .4266 times .3333 will have the following number of decimals in the product:
   A. 8　　B. 4　　C. 1　　D. None of these

4. An office floor is 25 ft. wide by 36 ft. long. To cover this floor with carpet will require _____ square yards.
   A. 100　　B. 300　　C. 900　　D. 25

5. 1/8 of 1% expressed as a decimal is
   A. .125　　B. .0125　　C. 1.25　　D. .00125

6. $\dfrac{6 \div 4}{6 \times 4}$ equals 6x4
   A. 1/16　　B. 1　　C. 1/6　　D. 1/4

7. 1/25 of 230 equals
   A. 92.0　　B. 9.20　　C. .920　　D. 920

8. 4 times 3/8 equals
   A. 1 3/8　　B. 3/32　　C. 12.125　　D. 1.5

9. 3/4 divided by 4 equals
   A. 3　　B. 3/16　　C. 16/3　　D. 16

10. 6/7 divided by 2/7 equals
    A. 6　　B. 12/49　　C. 3　　D. 21

11. The interest on $240 for 90 days ' 6% is
    A. $4.80　　B. $3.40　　C. $4.20　　D. $3.60

12. 16 2/3% of 1728 is
    A. 91　　B. 288　　C. 282　　D. 280

13. 6 1/4% of 6400 is   13.____
    A. 2500   B. 410   C. 108   D. 400

14. 12 1/2% of 560 is   14.____
    A. 65   B. 40   C. 50   D. 70

15. 2 yards divided by 3 equals   15.____
    A. 2 feet   B. 1/2 yard   C. 3 yards   D. 3 feet

16. A school has 540 pupils. 45% are boys. How many girls are there in this school?   16.____
    A. 243   B. 297   C. 493   D. 394

17. .1875 is equivalent to   17.____
    A. 18 3/4   B. 75/18   C. 18/75   D. 3/16

18. A kitchen cabinet listed at $42 is sold for $33.60. The discount allowed is   18.____
    A. 10%   B. 15%   C. 20%   D. 30%

19. 3 6/8 divided by 8 1/4 equals   19.____
    A. 9 1/8   B. 12   C. 5/11   D. 243.16

20. An agent sold goods to the amount of $1480. His commission at 5 1/2% was   20.____
    A. $37.50   B. $81.40   C. 76.70   D. $81.10

KEY (CORRECT ANSWERS

1.	C		11.	D
2.	B		12.	B
3.	A		13.	D
4.	A		14.	D
5.	D		15.	A
6.	A		16.	B
7.	B		17.	D
8.	D		18.	C
9.	B		19.	C
10.	C		20.	B

SOLUTIONS TO PROBLEMS

1. Let x = missing number. Then, 1600 = .40x. Solving, x = 4000

2. 2:05 PM - 9:15 AM = 4 hours 50 minutes

3. The product of two 4-decimal numbers is an 8-decimal number.

4. (25 ft)(36 ft) = 900 sq.ft. = 100 sq.yds.

5. (1/8)(1%) = (.125)(.01) = .00125

6. (6 ÷ 4) ÷ (6 x 4) = 3/2 ÷ 24 = (3/2)(1/24)= (1/16)

7. (1/25)(230) = 9.20

8. (4)(3/8) = 12/8 = 1.5

9. 3/4 ÷ 4 = (3/4)(1/4) = 3/16

10. 6/7 / 2/7 = (6/7)(7/2) = 3

11. ($240)(.06)(90/360) = $3.60

12. (16 2/3%)(1728) = (1/6)(1728) = 288

13. (6 1/4%)(6400) = (1/16)(6400) = 400

14. (12 1/2%)(560) = (1/8)(560) = 70

15. 2 yds ÷ 3 = 2/3 yds = (2/3)(3) = 2 ft.

16. If 45% are boys, then 55% are girls. Thus, (540)(.55) = 297

17. .1875 = 1875/10,000 = 3/16

18. $42 - $33.60 = $8.40.
    The discount is $8.40 ÷ $42 = .20 = 20%

19. 3 6/8 - 8 1/4 = (30/8)(4/33) = 5/11

20. ($1480)(.055) = $81.40

TEST 3

DIRECTIONS: Each question or incomplete statement is followed by several suggested answers or completions. Select the one that BEST answers the question or completes the statement. *PRINT THE LETTER OF THE CORRECT ANSWER IN THE SPACE AT THE RIGHT.*

1. 93.648 divided by 0.4 is

   A. 23.412   B. 234.12   C. 2.3412   D. 2341.2

   1.____

2. Add 4.3682, .0028, 34., 9.92, and from the sum subtract 1.992. The remainder is

   A. .46299   B. 4.6299   C. 462.99   D. 46.299

   2.____

3. At $2.88 per gross, three dozen will cost

   A. $8.64   B. $0.96   C. $0.72   D. $11.52

   3.____

4. 13 times 2.39 times 0.024 equals

   A. 745.68   B. 74.568   C. 7.4568   D. .74568

   4.____

5. A living room suite is marked $64 less 25 percent. A cash discount of 10 percent is allowed.
   The cash price is

   A. $53.20   B. $47.80   C. $36.00   D. $43.20

   5.____

6. 1/8 of 1 percent expressed as a decimal is

   A. .125   B. .0125   C. 1.25   D. .00125

   6.____

7. 16 percent of 482.11 equals

   A. 77.1376   B. 771.4240   C. 7714.2400   D. 7.71424

   7.____

8. A merchant sold a chair for $60. This was at a profit of 25 percent of what it cost him. The chair cost him

   A. $48   B. $45   C. $15   D. $75

   8.____

9. Add 5 hours 13 minutes, 3 hours 49 minutes, and 14 minutes. The sum is _____ hours _____ minutes.

   A. 9; 16   B. 9; 76   C. 8; 16   D. 8; 6

   9.____

10. 89 percent of $482 is

    A. $428.98   B. $472.36   C. $42.90   D. $47.24

    10.____

11. 200 percent of 800 is

    A. 16   B. 1600   C. 2500   D. 4

    11.____

12. Add 2 feet 3 inches, 4 feet 11 inches, 8 inches, 6 feet 6 inches. The sum is _____ feet _____ inches.

    A. 12; 4   B. 12; 14   C. 14; 4   D. 14; 28

    12.____

13. A merchant bought dresses at $15 each and sold them at $20 each. His overhead expenses are 20 percent of cost. His net profit on each dress is

    A. $1   B. $2   C. $3   D. $4

14. 0.0325 expressed as a percent is

    A. 325%   B. 3 1/4%   C. 32 1/2%   D. 32.5%

15. Add 3/4, 1/8, 1/32, 1/2; and from the sum subtract 4/8. The remainder is

    A. 2/32   B. 7/8   C. 29/32   D. 3/4

16. A salesman gets a commission of 4 percent on his sales. If he wants his commission to amount to $40, he will have to sell merchandise totaling

    A. $160   B. $10   C. $1,000   D. $100

17. Jones borrowed $225,000 for five years at 3 1/2 percent. The annual interest charge was

    A. $1,575   B. $1,555   C. $7,875   D. $39,375

18. A kitchen cabinet listed at $42 is sold for $33.60. The discount allowed is _____ percent.

    A. 10   B. 15   C. 20   D. 30

19. The exact number of days from May 5, 2007 to July 1, 2007 is _____ days.

    A. 59   B. 58   C. 56   D. 57

20. A dealer sells an article at a loss of 50% of the cost. Based on the selling price, the loss is

    A. 25%   B. 50%   C. 100%   D. none of these

KEY (CORRECT ANSWERS)

1. B   11. B
2. D   12. C
3. C   13. B
4. D   14. B
5. D   15. C
6. D   16. C
7. A   17. C
8. A   18. C
9. A   19. D
10. A   20. C

3 (#3)

SOLUTIONS TO PROBLEMS

1. $93.648 \div .4 = 234.12$

2. $4.368 + .0028 + 34 + 9.92 - 1.992 = 48.291 - 1.992 = 46.299$

3. $2.88 for 12 dozen means $.24 per dozen. Three dozen will cost (3)($.24) = $.72

4. $(13)(2.39)(.024) = .74568$

5. $(\$64)(.75)(.90) = \$43.20$

6. $(1/8)(1\%) = (.125)(.01) = .00125$

7. $(.16)(482.11) = 77.1376$

8. Let $x =$ cost. Then, $1.25x = \$60$. Solving, $x = \$48$

9. 5 hrs. 13 min. + 3 hrs. 49 min. + 14 min = 8 hrs. 76 min.

10. $(.89)(\$482) = \$428.98$

11. $200\% = 2$. So, $(200\%)(800) = (2)(800) = 1600$

12. 2 ft. 3 in. + 4 ft. 11 in. + 8 in. + 6 ft. 6 in. + 12 ft. 28 in. = 14 ft. 4 in.

13. Overhead is $(.20)(\$15) = \$3$. The net profit is $\$20 - \$15 - \$3 = \$2$

14. $.0325 = 3.25\% = 3\ 1/4\%$

15. $3/4 + 1/8 + 1/32 + 1/2 - 4/8 = 45/32 - 4/8 = 29/32$

16. Let $x =$ sales. Then, $\$40 = .04x$. Solving, $x = \$1000$

17. Annual interest is $(\$225,000)(.035) \times 1 = 7875$

18. $\$42 - \$33.60 = \$8.40$. Then, $\$8.40 \div \$42 = .20 = 20\%$

19. The number of days left for May, June, July is 26, 30, and 1. Thus, $26 + 30 + 1 = 57$

20. Let $x =$ cost, so that $.50x =$ selling price. The loss is represented by $.50x \div .50x = 1 = 100\%$ on the selling price. (Note: The loss in dollars is $x - .50x = .50x$)

ARITHMETIC
EXAMINATION SECTION
TEST 1

DIRECTIONS: Each question or incomplete statement is followed by several suggested answers or completions. Select the one that BEST answers the question or completes the statement. *PRINT THE LETTER OF TEE CORRECT ANSWER IN THE SPACE AT THE RIGHT.*

1. Add $4.34, $34.50, $6.00, $101.76, $90.67. From the result, subtract $60.54 and $10,56. 1.____
   A. $76.17   B. $156.37   C. $166.17   D. $300.37

2. Add 2,200, 2,600, 252 and 47.96. From the result, subtract 202.70, 1,200, 2,150 and 434.43. 2.____
   A. 1,112.83   B. 1,213.46   C. 1,341.51   D. 1,348.91

3. Multiply 1850 by .05 and multiply 3300 by .08 and, then, add both results, 3.____
   A. 242.50   B. 264,00   C. 333.25   D. 356.50

4. Multiply 312.77 by .04. Round off the result to the nearest hundredth. 4.____
   A. 12.52   B. 12.511   C. 12.518   D. 12.51

5. Add 362.05, 91.13, 347.81 and 17.46 and then divide the result by 6. The answer, rounded off to the nearest hundredth, is: 5.____
   A. 138.409   B. 137.409   C. 136.41   D. 136.40

6. Add 66.25 and 15.06 and, then, multiply the result by 2 1/6. The answer is, most nearly, 6.____
   A. 176.18   B. 176.17   C. 162.66   D. 162.62

7. Each of the following items contains three decimals. In which case do *all* three decimals have the SAME value? 7.____
   A. .3; .30; .03   B. .25; .250; .2500
   C. 1.9; 1.90; 1.09   D. .35; .350; .035

8. Add 1/2 the sum of (539.84 and 479.26) to 1/3 the sum of (1461.93 and 927.27). Round off the result to the nearest whole number. 8.____
   A. 3408   B. 2899   C. 1816   D. 1306

9. Multiply $5,906.09 by 15% and, then, divide the result by 3 and round off to the nearest cent. 9.____
   A. $295.30   B. $885.91   C. $2,657.74   D. $29,530.45

10. Multiply 630 by 517. 10.____
    A. 325,710   B. 345,720   C. 362,425   D. 385,660

97

11. Multiply 35 by 846. 11.____
    A. 4050   B. 9450   C. 18740   D. 29610

12. Multiply 823 by 0.05. 12.____
    A. 0.4115   B. 4.115   C. 41.15   D. 411.50

13. Multiply 1690 by 0.10. 13.____
    A. 0.169   B. .1.69   C. 16.90   D. 169.0

14. Divide 2765 by 35. 14.____
    A. 71   B. 79   C. 87   D. 93

15. From $18.55 subtract $6.80. 15.____
    A. $9.75   B. $10.95   C. $11.75   D. $25.35

16. The sum of 2.75 + 4.50 + 3.60 is: 16.____
    A. 9.75   B. 10.85   C. 11.15   D. 11.95

17. The sum of 9.63 + 11.21 + 17.25 is: 17.____
    A. 36.09   B. 38.09   C. 39.92   D. 41.22

18. The sum of 112.0 + 16.9 + 3.84 is: 18.____
    A. 129.3   B. 132.74   C. 136.48   D. 167.3

19. When 65 is added to the result of 14 multiplied by 13, the answer is: 19.____
    A. 92   B. 182   C. 247   D. 16055

20. From $391.55 subtract $273.45. 20.____
    A. $118.10   B. $128.20   C. $178.10   D. $218.20

KEY (CORRECT ANSWERS)

1.	C	11.	D
2.	A	12.	C
3.	D	13.	D
4.	D	14.	B
5.	C	15.	C
6.	B	16.	B
7.	B	17.	B
8.	D	18.	B
9.	C	19.	C
10.	A	20.	A

SOLUTIONS TO PROBLEMS

1. ($4.34 + $34.50 + $6.00 + $101.76 + $90.67) - ($60.54 + $10.56) = $237.27 - $71.10 = $166.17.

2. (2200 + 2600 + 252 + 47.96) - (202.70 + 1200 + 2150 + 434.43) = 5099.96 - 3987.13 = 1112.83

3. (1850)(.05) + (3300)(.08) = 92.5 + 264 = 356.50

4. (312.77)(.04) = 12.5108 = 12.51 to nearest hundredth

5. $(362.05 + 91.13 + 347.81 + 17.46) \div 6 = 136.40\overline{83} = 136.41$ to nearest hundredth

6. $(66.25 + 15.06)(2\frac{1}{6}) = 176.171\overline{6} \approx 176.17$

7. .25 = .250 = .2500

8. $(\frac{1}{2})(539.84 + 479.26) + \frac{1}{3}(1461.93 + 927.27) = 509.55 + 796.4 = 1305.95 = 1306$ nearest whole number

9. ($5906.09)(.15) ÷ 3 = ($885.9135)/3 = 295.3045 = $295.30 to nearest cent

10. (630)(517) = 325,710

11. (35)(846) = 29,610

12. (823)(.05) = 41.15

13. (1690)(10) = 169.0

14. 2765 ÷ 3.5 = 79

15. $18.55 - $6.80 = $11.75

16. 2.75 + 4.50 + 3.60 = 10.85

17. 9.63 + 11.21 + 17.25 = 38.09

18. 112.0 + 16.9 + 3.84 = 132.74

19. 65 + (14)(13) = 65 + 182 = 247

20. $391.55 - $273.45 = $118.10

TEST 2

DIRECTIONS   Each question or incomplete statement is followed by several suggested answers or completions. Select the one that BEST answers the question or completes the statement. PRINT THE LETTER OF TEE CORRECT ANSWER IN THE SPACE AT THE RIGHT.

1. The sum of $29.61 + $101.53 + $943.64 is: 1.____
   A. $983.88   B. $1074.78   C. $1174.98   D. $1341.42

2. The sum of $132.25 + $85.63 + $7056,44 is: 2.____
   A. $1694.19   B. $7274.32   C. $8464.57   D. $9346.22

3. The sum of 4010 + 1271 + 838 + 23 is: 3.____
   A. 6142   B. 6162   C. 6242   D. 6362

4. The sum of 53632 + 27403 + 98765 + 75424 is: 4.____
   A. 19214   B. 215214   C. 235224   D. 255224

5. The sum of 76342 + 49050 + 21206 + 59989 is: 5.____
   A. 196586   B. 206087   C. 206587   D. 234487

6. The sum of $452.13 + $963.45 + $621.25 is: 6.____
   A. $1936.83   B. $2036.83   C. $2095.73   D. $2135.73

7. The sum of 36392 + 42156 + 98765 is: 7.____
   A. 167214   B. 177203   C. 177313   D. 178213

8. The sum of 40125 + 87123 + 24689 is: 8.____
   A. 141827   B. 151827   C. 151937   D. 161947

9. The sum of 2379 + 4015 + 6521 + 9986 is: 9.____
   A. 22901   B. 22819   C. 21801   D. 21791

10. From 50962 subtract 36197. 10.____
    A. 14675   B. 14765   C. 14865   D. 24765

11. From 90000 subtract 31928. 11.____
    A. 58072   B. 59062   C. 68172   D. 69182

12. From 63764 subtract 21548. 12.____
    A. 42216   B. 43122   C. 45126   D. 85312

13. From $9605.13 subtract $2715.96. 13.____
    A. $12,321.09   B. $8,690.16   C. $6,990.07   D. $6,889.17

14. From 76421 subtract 73101.   14.____
    A. 3642   B. 3540   C. 3320   D. 3242

15. From $8.25 subtract $6.50.   15.____
    A. $1.25   B. $1.50   C. $1.75   D. $2.25

16. Multiply 583 by 0.50.   16.____
    A. $291.50 B. 28.15   C. 2.815   D. 0.2815

17. Multiply 0.35 by 1045.   17.____
    A. 0.36575 B. 3.6575 C. 36.575 D. 365.75

18. Multiply 25 by 2513.   18.____
    A. 62825   B. 62725   C. 60825   D. 52825

19. Multiply 423 by 0.01.   19.____
    A. 0.0423 B. 0.423   C. 4.23   D. 42.3

20. Multiply 6.70 by 3.2.   20.____
    A. 2.1440 B. 21.440 C. 214.40 D. 2144.0

KEY (CORRECT ANSWERS)

1. B   11. A
2. B   12. A
3. A   13. D
4. D   14. C
5. C   15. C

6. B   16. A
7. C   17. D
8. C   18. A
9. A   19. C
10. B   20. B

3 (#2)

SOLUTIONS TO PROBLEMS

1. $29.61 + $101.53 + $943.64 = $1074.78

2. $132.25 + $85.63 + $7056.44 = $7274.32

3. 4010 + 1271 + 838 + 23 = 6142

4. 53,632 + 27,403 + 98,765 + 75,424 = 255,224

5. 76,342 + 49,050 + 21,206 + 59,989 = 206,587

6. $452.13 + $963.45 + $621.25 = $2036.83

7. 36,392 + 42,156 + 98,765 = 177,313

8. 40,125 + 87,123 + 24,689 = 151,937

9. 2379 + 4015 + 6521 + 9986 = 22,901

10. 50962 - 36197 = 14,765

11. 90,000 - 31,928 = 58,072

12. 63,764 - 21,548 = 42,216

13. $9605.13 - $2715.96 = $6889.17

14. 76,421 - 73,101 = 3320

15. $8.25 - $6.50 = $1.75

16. (583)(.50) = 291.50

17. (.35)(1045) = 365.75

18. (25)(2513) = 62,825

19. (423)(.01) = 4.23

20. (6.70)(3.2) = 21.44

TEST 3

DIRECTIONS: Each question or incomplete statement is followed by several suggested answers or completions. Select the one that *BEST* answers the question or completes the statement. *PRINT THE LETTER OF TEE CORRECT ANSWER IN THE SPACE AT THE RIGHT.*

Questions 1-4.

DIRECTIONS: For each of Questions 1-4, perform the indicated arithmetic and choose the correct answer from among the four choices given.

1. 12.485
   + 347

   A. 12,038   B. 12,128   C. 12,782   D. 12,832

2. 74,137
   + 711

   A. 74,326   B. 74,848   C. 78,028   D. .D. 78,926

3. 3,749
   - 671

   A. 3,078   B. 3,168   C. 4,028   D. 4,420

4. 19,805
   -18904

   A. 109   B. 901   C. 1,109   D. 1,901

5. When 119 is subtracted from the sum of 2016 + 1634, the remainder is:

   A. 2460   B. 3531   C. 3650   D. 3769

6. Multiply 35 X 65 X 15.

   A. 2275   B. 24265   C. 31145   D. 34125

7. 90% expressed as a decimal is:

   A. .009   B. .09   C. .9   D. 9.0

8. Seven-tenths of a foot expressed in inches is:

   A. 5.5   B. 6.5   C. 7   D. 8.4

9. If 95 men were divided into crews of five men each, the *number* of crews that will be formed is:

   A. 16   B. 17   C. 18   D. 19

10. If a man earns $19.50 an hour, the *number* of working hours it will take him to earn $4,875 is, most nearly,

    A. 225 B. 250 C. 275 D. 300

11. If 5 1/2 loads of gravel cost $55.00, then 6 1/2 loads will cost:

    A. $60. B. $62.50 C. $65. D. $66.00

12. At $2.50 a yard, 27 yards of concrete will cost:

    A. $36. B. $41.80 C. $54. D. $67.50

13. A distance is measured and found to be 52.23 feet. In feet and inches, this distance is, most nearly, 52 feet *and*

    A. 2 3/4" B. 3 1/4" C. 3 3/4" D. 4 1/4"

14. If a maintainer gets $5.20 per hour and time and one-half for working over 40 hours, his *gross* salary for a week in which he worked 43 hours would be

    A. $208.00 B. $223.60 C. $231.40 D. $335.40

15. The circumference of a circle is given by the formula $C = \Pi D$, where C is the circumference, D is the diameter, and Π is about 3 1/7.
    If a coil is 15 turns of steel cable has an average diameter of 20 inches, the *total* length of cable on the coil is *nearest to*

    A. 5 feet B. 78 feet C. 550 feet D. 943 feet

16. The measurements of a poured concrete foundation show that 54 cubic feet of concrete have been placed.
    If payment for this concrete is to be on the basis of cubic yards, the 54 cubic feet must be

    A. multiplied by 27   B. multiplied by 3
    C. divided by 27   D. divided by 3

17. If the cost of 4 1/2 tons of structural steel is $1,800, then the cost of 12 tons is, most nearly,

    A. $4,800 B. $5,400 C. $7,200 D. $216,000

18. An hourly-paid employee working 12:00 midnight to 8:00 a.m. is directed to report to the medical staff for a physical examination at 11:00 a.m. of the same day.
    The pay allowed him for reporting will be an extra

    A. 1 hour B. 2 hours C. 3 hours D. 4 hours

19. The *total* length of four pieces of 2" pipe, whose lengths are 7' 3 1/2", 4' 2 3/16", 5' 7 5/16", and 8' 5 7/8", respectively, is:

    A. 24' 6 3/4"   B. 24' 7 15/16"
    C. 25' 5 13/16"   D. 25' 6 7/8"

20. As a senior mortuary caretaker, you are preparing a monthly report, using the following figures: 20.____

    No. of bodies received   983
    No. of bodies claimed   720
    No. of bodies sent to city cemetery   14
    No. of bodies sent to medical schools   9

How many bodies remained at the end of the monthly reporting period?

   A. 230   B. 240   C. 250   D. 260

KEY (CORRECT ANSWERS)

1.	D	11.	C
2.	B	12.	D
3.	A	13.	A
4.	B	14.	C
5.	B	15.	B
6.	D	16.	C
7.	C	17.	A
8.	D	18.	C
9.	D	19.	D
10.	B	20.	B

SOLUTIONS TO PROBLEMS

1. 12,485 + 347 = 12,832

2. 74,137 + 711 = 74,848

3. 3749 - 671 = 3078

4. 19,805 - 18,904 = 901

5. (2016 + 1634) - 119 = 3650 - 119 = 3531

6. (35)(65)(15) = 34,125

7. 90% = .90 or .9

8. $(\frac{7}{10})(12) = 8.4$ inches

9. 95 ÷ 5 = 19 crews

10. $4875 ÷ $19.50 = 250 days

11. Let x = cost. Then, $\frac{5\frac{1}{2}}{6\frac{1}{2}} = \frac{\$55.00}{x}$. $5\frac{1}{2} = 357.50$. Solving, x = $65

12. ($2.50)(27) = $67.50

13. .23-ft. = 2.76 in., so 52.23 ft $\approx$ 52 ft. $2\frac{3}{4}$ in. $(.76 \approx \frac{3}{4})$

14. Salary = ($5.20)(40) + ($7.80)(3) = $231.40

15. Length $\approx (15)(3\frac{1}{7})(20) \approx 943$ in. ≈ 78 ft.

16. There are 27 cu.ft. in 1 cu.yd. To change from 54 cu.ft. to cu.yds., divide by 27.

17. $1800 ÷ $4\frac{1}{2}$ = = $400 per ton. Then, 12 tons cost ($400)(12) = $4800

18. Instead of working 12 to 8, he will be staying until 11 AM, an extra 3 hours.

19. $7'3\frac{1}{2}" + 4'2\frac{3}{16}" + 5'7\frac{5}{16}" + 8'5\frac{7}{8}" = 24'17\frac{30}{16}" = 24'18\frac{7}{8}"$

20. 983 - 720 - 14 - 9 = 240 bodies left.

ARITHMETICAL REASONING

EXAMINATION SECTION

TEST 1

DIRECTIONS: Each question or incomplete statement is followed by several suggested answers or completions. Select the one that BEST answers the question or completes the statement. *PRINT THE LETTER OF THE CORRECT ANSWER IN THE SPACE AT THE RIGHT.*

1. The ABC Corporation had a gross income of $125,500.00 in 2019. Of this, it paid 60% for overhead.
   If the gross income for 2020 increased by $6,500 and the cost of overhead increased to 61% of gross income, how much MORE did it pay for overhead in 2020 than in 2019?
   A. $1,320   B. $5,220   C. $7,530   D. $8,052

   1._____

2. After one year, Mr. Richards paid back a total of $16,950 as payment for a $15,000 loan. All the money paid over $15,000 was simple interest.
   The interest charge was MOST NEARLY
   A. 13%   B. 11%   C. 9%   D. 7%

   2._____

3. A checking account has a balance of $253.36.
   If deposits of $36.95, $210.23, and $7.34 and withdrawals of $117.35, $23.37, and $15.98 are made, what is the NEW balance of the account?
   A. $155.54   B. $351.18   C. $364.58   D. $664.58

   3._____

4. In 2020, the W Realty Company spent 27% of its income on rent.
   If it earned $97,254 in 2020, the amount it paid for rent was
   A. $26,258.58   B. 26,348.58   C. $27,248.58   D. $27,358.58

   4._____

5. Six percent simple annual interest on $2,436.18 is MOST NEARLY
   A. $145.08   B. $145.17   C. $146.08   D. $146.17

   5._____

6. H. Partridge receives a weekly gross salary (before deductions) of $397.50. Through weekly payroll deductions of $13.18, he is paying back a loan he took from his pension fund.
   If other fixed weekly deductions amount to $122.76, how much pay would Mr. Partridge take home over a period of 33 weeks?
   A. $7,631.28   B. $8,250.46   C. $8,631.48   D. $13,117.50

   6._____

7. Mr. Robertson is a city employee enrolled in a city retirement system. He has taken out a loan from the retirement fund and is paying it back at the rate of $14.90 every two weeks.
   In eighteen weeks, how much money will he have paid back on the loan?
   A. $268.20   B. $152.80   C. $134.10   D. $67.05

   7._____

8. In 2019, The Iridor Book Company had the following expenses: rent, $6,500; overhead, $52,585; inventory, $35,700; and miscellaneous, $1,275.
   If all of these expenses went up 18% in 2020, what would they TOTAL in 2020?
   A. $17,290.80   B. $78,769.20   C. $96,060.00   D. $113,350.80

9. Ms. Ranier had a gross salary of $710.72 paid once every two weeks.
   If the deductions from each paycheck are $125.44, $50.26, $12.58, and $2.54, how much money would Ms. Ranier take home in eight weeks?
   A. $2,079.60   B. $2,842.88   C. $4,159.20   D. $5,685.76

10. Mr. Martin had a net income of $95,500 in 2019.
    If he spent 34% on rent and household expenses, 3% on house furnishings, 25% on clothes, and 36% on food, how much was left for savings and other expenses?
    A. $980   B. $1,910   C. $3,247   D. $9,800

11. Mr. Elsberg can pay back a loan of $1,800 from the city employees' retirement system if he pays back $36.69 every two weeks for two full years.
    At the end of the two years, how much more than the original $1,800 he borrowed will Mr. Elsberg have paid back?
    A. $53.94   B. $107.88   C. $190.79   D. $214.76

12. Mr. Nusbaum is a city employee receiving a gross salary (salary before deductions) of $20,800. Every two weeks, the following deductions are taken out of his salary: Federal Income Tax, $162.84; FICA, $44.26; State Tax, $29.2; City Tax, $13.94; Health Insurance, $3.14.
    If Mr. Nusbaum's salary and deductions remained the same for a full calendar year, what would his net salary (gross salary less deductions) be in that year?
    A. $6,596.20   B. $14,198.60   C. $18,745.50   D. $20,546.30

13. Add: 8936, 7821, 8953, 4297, 9785, 6579.
    A. 45,371   B. 45,381   C. 46,371   D. 46,381

14. Multiply: 987
              867
    A. 854,609   B. 854,729   C. 855,709   D. 855,729

15. Divide: 59)321439.0
    A. 5438.1   B. 5447.1   C. 5448.1   D. 5457.1

16. Divide: .052)721
    A. 12,648.0   B. 12,648.1   C. 12,649.0   D. 12,649.1

17. If the total number of employees in one city agency increased from 1,927 to 2,006 during a certain year, the percentage increase in the number of employees for that year is MOST NEARLY
    A. 4%   B. 5%   C. 6%   D. 7%

18. During a single fiscal year, which totaled 248 workdays, one account clerk verified 1,488 purchase vouchers.
Assuming a normal work week of five days, what is the AVERAGE number of vouchers verified by the account clerk in a one-week period during this fiscal year?
   A. 25   B. 30   C. 35   D. 40

18._____

19. Multiplying a number by .75 is the same as
   A. multiplying it by $2/3$
   B. dividing it by $2/3$
   C. multiplying it by $3/4$
   D. dividing it by $3/4$

19._____

20. In City Agency A, $2/3$ of the employees are enrolled in a retirement system. City Agency B has the same number of employees as Agency A and 60% of these are enrolled in a retirement system.
If Agency A has a total of 660 employees, how many MORE employees does it have enrolled in a retirement system than does Agency B?
   A. 36   B. 44   C. 56   D. 66

20._____

21. Net worth is equal to assets minus liabilities.
If, at the end of 2019, a textile company had assets of $98,695.83 and liabilities of $59,238.29, what was its net worth?
   A. $38,478.54   B. $38,488.64   C. $39,457.54   D. $48,557.54

21._____

22. Mr. Martin's assets consist of the following: Cash on hand, $5,233.74; Automobile, $3,206.09; Furniture, $4,925.00; Government Bonds, $5,500.00; and House, $36,69.85.
What are his TOTAL assets?
   A. $54,545.68   B. $54,455.68   C. $55,455.68   D. $55,555.68

22._____

23. If Mr. Mitchell has $627.04 in his checking account and then writes three checks for $241.75, $13.24, and $102.97, what will be his new balance?
   A. $257.88   B. $269.08   C. $357.96   D. $369.96

23._____

24. An employee's net pay is equal to his total earnings less all deductions.
If an employee's total earnings in a pay period are $497.05, what is his net pay if he has the following deductions: Federal Income Tax, $18.79; City Tax, $7.25; Pension, $1.88?
   A. $351.17   B. $351.07   C. $350.17   D. $350.07

24._____

25. A petty cash fund had an opening balance of $85.75 on December 1. Expenditures of $23.00, $15.65, $5.23, $14.75, and $26.38 were made out of this fund during the first 14 days of the month. Then, on December 17, another $38.50 was added to the fund.
If additional expenditures of $17.18, $3.29, and $11.64 were made during the remainder of the month, what was the FINAL balance of the petty cash fund at the end of December?
   A. $6.93   B. $7.13   C. $46.51   D. $91.40

25._____

KEY (CORRECT ANSWERS)

1.	B		11.	B
2.	A		12.	B
3.	B		13.	C
4.	A		14.	D
5.	D		15.	C
6.	C		16.	D
7.	C		17.	A
8.	D		18.	B
9.	A		19.	C
10.	B		20.	B

21.	C
22.	D
23.	B
24.	D
25.	B

5 (#1)

SOLUTIONS TO PROBLEMS

1. ($132,000)(.61) − ($125,500)(.60) = $5,220

2. Interest = $1,950. As a percent, $1950 ÷ 15,000 = 13%

3. New balance = $253.36 + $36.95 + $210.23 + $7.34 - $117.35 - $23.37 - $15.98 = $351.18

4. Rent = ($97,254)(.27) = $26,258.58

5. ($2,436.18)(.06) ≈ $146.17

6. ($397.50 - $13.18 - $122.76) = $8,631.48

7. ($14.90)($\frac{18}{2}$) = $134.10

8. ($6,500 + $52,585 + $35,700 + $1,275)(1.18) = $113,350.80

9. ($710.72 - $125.44 - $50.26 - $12.58 - $2.54)($\frac{8}{2}$) = $2,079.60

10. (1 - .34 - .03 - .25 - .36) - $1,800 = $107.88

11. (36.69)(52) - $1,800 = $107.88

12. $20,800 − (26)($162.84+$44.26+$29.72+$13.94+$3.14) = $14,198.60

13. 8,936 + 7,821 + 8,953 + 4,297 + 9,785 + 6,579 = 46,371

14. (987)(867) − 855,729

15. 321,439 ÷ 59 ≈ 5,448.1

16. 721 ÷ .057 ≈ 12,649.1

17. (2,006-1,927) ÷ 1,927 ≈ 4%

18. Let x = number of vouchers. Then, $\frac{x}{5} = \frac{1488}{248}$. Solving, x = 30

19. Multiplying by .75 is equivalent to multiplying by $\frac{3}{4}$

20. (660)($\frac{2}{3}$) − (660)(.60) = 44

21. Net worth = $98,695.83 - $59,238.29 = $39,457.54

6 (#1)

22. Total Assets = $5,233.74 + $3,206.09 + $4,925.00 + $5,500.00) + $36,690.85 = $55,555.68.

23. New balance = $627.04 - $241.75 - $13.24 - $102.97 = $269.08

24. Net pay = $497.05 - $90.32 - $28.74 - $18.79 - $7.25 - $1.88 = $350.07

25. Final balance = $85.75 - $23.00 - $15.65 - $5.23 - $14.75 - $26.38 + $38.50 - $17.18 - $3.29 - $11.64 = $7.13

TEST 2

DIRECTIONS: Each question or incomplete statement is followed by several suggested answers or completions. Select the one that BEST answers the question or completes the statement. *PRINT THE LETTER OF THE CORRECT ANSWER IN THE SPACE AT THE RIGHT.*

1. The formula for computing base salary is: Earnings equals base gross plus additional gross.
   If an employee's earnings during a particular period are in the amounts of $597.45, $535.92, $639.91, and $552.83, and his base gross salary is $525.50 per paycheck, what is the TOTAL of the additional gross earned by the employee during that period?
   A. $224.11 B. $224.21 C. $224.51 D. $244.11

2. If a lump sum death benefit is paid by the retirement system in an amount equal to 3/7 of an employee's last yearly salary of $13,486.50, the amount of the death benefit paid is MOST NEARLY
   A. $5,749.29 B. $5,759.92 C. $5,779.92 D. $5,977.29

3. Suppose that a member has paid 15 installments on a 28-installment loan. The percentage of the number of installments paid to the retirement system is
   A. 53.57% B. 53.97% C. 54.57% D. 55.37%

4. If an employee takes a 1-month vacation during a calendar year, the percentage of the year during which he works is MOST NEARLY
   A. 90.9% B. 91.3% C. 91.6% D. 92.1%

5. Suppose that an employee took a leave of absence totaling 7 months during a calendar year.
   Assuming the employee did not take any vacation time during the remainder of that year, the percentage of the year in which he worked is MOST NEARLY
   A. 41.7% B. 43.3% C. 46.5% D. 47.1%

6. A member has borrowed $4,725 from her funds in the retirement system. If $3,213 has been repaid, the percentage of the loan which is still outstanding is MOST NEARLY
   A. 16% B. 32% C. 48% D. 68%

7. If an employee worked only 24 weeks during the year because of illness, the portion of the year he was out of work was MOST NEARLY
   A. 46% B. 48% C. 51% D. 54%

8. If an employee purchased credit for a 16-week period of service which he had prior to rejoining the retirement system, the percentage of a year he purchased credit for was MOST NEARLY
   A. 27.9% B. 28.8% C. 30.7% D. 33.3%

1.____
2.____
3.____
4.____
5.____
6.____
7.____
8.____

9. If an employee contributes 2/11 of his yearly salary to his pension fund account, the percentage of his yearly salary which he contributes is MOST NEARLY
   A. 17.9%   B. 18.2%   C. 18.4%   D. 19.0%

10. In 2018, the maximum amount of income from which social security tax could be withheld (base salary) was $70,500. In 2020, the base salary was $82,500. The 2020 base salary represents a percentage increase over the 2018 base salary of APPROXIMATELY
    A. 15%   B. 16%   C. 17%   D. 18%

11. If 17.5% of an employee's salary is withheld for taxes, the one of the following which is the fraction of the salary withheld is
    A. 3/20   B. 8/35   C. 7/40   D. 4/25

12. If a person withdraws 42% of the funds from his account with the retirement system, the remaining balance represents a fraction of MOST NEARLY
    A. 7/13   B. 5/9   C. 7/12   D. 4/7

13. A property decreases in value from $45,000 to $35,000. The percent of decrease is MOST NEARLY
    A. 20.5%   B. 22.2%   C. 25.0%   D. 28.6%

14. The fraction $\frac{487}{101326}$ expressed as a decimal is MOST NEARLY
    A. .0482   B. .00481   C. .0049   D. .00392

15. The reciprocal of the sum of 2/3 and 1/6 can be expressed as
    A. 0.83   B. 1.20   C. 1.25   D. 1.50

16. Total land and building costs for a new commercial property equal $50 per square foot.
    If the investors expect a 10 percent return on their costs, and if total operating expenses average 5 percent of total costs, annual gross rentals per square foot must be AT LEAST
    A. $7.50   B. $8.50   C. $10.00   D. $12.00

17. The formula for computing the amount of annual deposit in a compound interest bearing account to provide a lump sum at the end of a period of years is
    $X = \frac{r \cdot L}{(1+r)^{n-1}}$ (X is the amount of annual deposit, r is the rate of interest, and n is the number of years and L = lump sum).
    Using the formula, the annual amount of the deposit at the end of each year to accumulate $20,000 at the end of 3 years with interest at 2 percent on annual balances is
    A. $6,120.00   B. $6,203.33   C. $6,535.09   D. $6,666.66

3 (#2)

18. An investor sold two properties at $150,000 each. On one he made a 2.5 percent profit. On the other, he suffered a 25 percent loss.
The NET result of his sales was
   A. neither a gain nor a loss
   B. a $20,000 loss
   C. a $75,000 gain
   D. a $75,000 loss

18.____

19. A contractor decides to install a chain fence covering the perimeter of a parcel 75 feet wide and 112 feet in depth.
Which one of the following represents the number of feet to be covered?
   A. 187   B. 364   C. 374   D. 8,400

19.____

20. A builder estimates he can build an average of 4½ one-family homes to an acre. There are 640 acres to one square mile.
Which one of the following CORRECTLY represents the number of one-family homes the builder would estimate he can build on one square mile?
   A. 1,280   B. 1,920   C. 2,560   D. 2,880

20.____

21. $.01059 deposit at 7 percent interest will yield $1.00 in 30 years.
If a person deposited $1,059 at 7 percent interest on April 4, 1991, which one of the following amounts would represent the worth of this deposit on March 31, 2021?
   A. $100   B. $1,000   C. $10,000   D. $100,000

21.____

22. A building has an economic life of forty years.
Assuming the building depreciates at a constant annual rate, which one of the following CORRECTLY represents the yearly percentage of depreciation?
   A. 2.0%   B. 2.5%   C. 5.0%   D. 7.0%

22.____

23. A building produces a gross income of $200,000 with a net income of $20,000, before mortgage charges and capital recapture. The owner is able to increase the gross income 5 percent without a corresponding increase in operating costs.
The effect upon the net income will be an INCREASE of
   A. 5%   B. 10%   C. 12.5%   D. 50%

23.____

24. The present value of $1.00 not payable for 8 years, and at 10 percent interest, is $.4665.
Which of the following amounts represents the PRESENT value of $1,000 payable 8 years hence at 10 percent interest?
   A. $46.65   B. $466.50   C. $4,665.00   D. $46,650.00

24.____

25. The amount of real property taxes to be levied by a city is $100 million. The assessment roll subject to taxation shows an assessed valuation of $2 billion.
Which one of the following tax rates CORRECTLY represents the tax rate to be levied per $100 of assessed valuation?
   A. $.50   B. $5.00   C. $50.00   D. $500.00

25.____

KEY (CORRECT ANSWERS)

1.	A		11.	C
2.	C		12.	C
3.	A		13.	B
4.	C		14.	B
5.	A		15.	B
6.	B		16.	A
7.	D		17.	C
8.	C		18.	B
9.	B		19.	C
10.	C		20.	D

21. D
22. B
23. D
24. B
25. B

5 (#2)

SOLUTIONS TO PROBLEMS

1. $597.45 + $535.91 + $639.91 + $552.83 = $2,326.11. Then, $2,326.11 − (4)($525.50) = $224.11

2. Death benefit = ($13,486.50)$(\frac{3}{7})$ ≈ $5,779.92

3. $\frac{15}{28}$ ≈ 53.57%

4. $\frac{11}{12}$ ≈ 91.6% (closer to 91.7%)

5. $\frac{5}{12}$ ≈ 41.7%

6. ($4,725−$3,213) ÷ $4,725 = 32%

7. $\frac{28}{52}$ ≈ 54%

8. $\frac{16}{52}$ ≈ 30.7% (closer to 30.8%)

9. $\frac{2}{11}$ ≈ 18.2%

10. ($82,500 − $70,500) ÷ $70,500 = 17%

11. 17.5% = $\frac{175}{1000}$ = $\frac{7}{40}$

12. 100% − 42% = 58% = $\frac{58}{100}$ = $\frac{29}{50}$, closest to $\frac{7}{12}$ in selections

13. $\frac{\$10,000}{\$45,000}$ ≈ 22.2%

14. 487/101,216 ≈ .00481

15. $\frac{2}{3} + \frac{1}{6} = \frac{5}{6}$ Then, $1 \div \frac{5}{6} = \frac{6}{5}$ = 1.20

16. (.15)($50) = $7.50

17. x = (.02)($20,000)/[(1+.02)^3 − 1] = 400 ÷ .061208 ≈ $6,535.09

18. Sold 150,000, 25% loss = paid 200,000, loss of $50,000 Sold 150,000, 25% profit = paid 120,000, profit of 30,000 − 50,000 + 30,000 = 20,000 (loss)

19. Perimeter = (2)(75) + (2)(112) = 374 ft.

20. (640)(4½) = 2,880 homes

21. (1÷.01059)(1059) = $100,000

22. 1÷4 = .025 = 2.5%

23. New gross income = ($200,000)(X1.05) = $210,000
    Then, ($210,000-$200,000) ÷ $20,000 = 50%

24. Let x = present value of $1,000. Then, $\frac{\$1.00}{\$.4665} = \frac{\$1000}{x}$
    Solving, x = $466.50

25. Let x = tax rate. Then, $\frac{\$100,000,000}{\$2,000,000,000} = \frac{x}{\$100}$
    Solving, x = $5.00

TEST 3

DIRECTIONS: Each question or incomplete statement is followed by several suggested answers or completions. Select the one that BEST answers the question or completes the statement. *PRINT THE LETTER OF THE CORRECT ANSWER IN THE SPACE AT THE RIGHT.*

1. It is found that for the past three years the average weekly number of inspections per inspector ranged from 20 inspections to 40 inspections.
   On the basis of this information, it is MOST reasonable to conclude that
   A. on the average, 30 inspections per week were made
   B. the average weekly number of inspections never fell below 20
   C. the performance of inspectors deteriorated over the three-year period
   D. the range in average weekly inspections was 60

1.____

Questions 2-4.

DIRECTIONS: Questions 2 through 4 are to be answered on the basis of the following information.

The number of students admitted to University X in 2019 from High School Y was 268 students. This represented 13.7 percent of University X's entering freshman classes. In 2020, it is expected that University X will admit 591 students from High School Y, which is expected to represent 19.4 percent of the 2020 entering freshman classes of University X.

2. Which of the following is CLOSEST estimate of the size of University's expected 2020 entering freshman classes?
   _____ students
   A. 2,000   B. 2,500   C. 3,000   D. 3,500

2.____

3. Of the following, the expected percentage of increase from 2019 to 2020 in the number of students graduating from High School Y and entering University X as freshmen is MOST NEARLY
   A. 5.7%   B. 20%   C. 45%   D. 120%

3.____

4. Assume that the cost of processing admission to University X from High School Y in 2019 was an average of $28. Also, that this was 1/3 more than the average cost of processing each of the other 2019 freshmen admissions to University X.
   Then, the one of the following that MOST closely shows the total processing cost of all 2019 freshman admissions to University X is
   A. $6,500   B. $20,000   C. $30,000   D. $40,000

4.____

5. Assume that during the fiscal year 2019-2020, a bureau produced 20% more work units than it produced in the fiscal year 2018-2019. Also assume that during the fiscal year 2019-2020 that bureau's staff was 20% smaller than it was in the fiscal year 2018-2019.

5.____

119

On the basis of this information, it would be MOST proper to conclude that the number of work units produced per staff member in that bureau in the fiscal year 2019-2020 exceeded the number of work units produced per staff member in that bureau in the fiscal year 2018-2019 by which one of the following percentages?
A. 20%   B. 25%   C. 40%   D. 50%

6. Assume that during the following fiscal years (FY), a bureau has received the following appropriations:
 FY 2015-2016 - $200,000
 FY 2016-2017 - $240,000
 FY 2017-2018 - $280,000
 FY 2018-2019 - $390,000
 FY 2019-2020 - $505,000

 The bureau's appropriation for which one of the following fiscal years showed the LARGEST percentage of increase over the bureau's appropriation for the immediately previous fiscal year?
 A. FY 2016-2017
 B. FY 2017-2018
 C. FY 2018-2019
 D. FY 2010-2020

7. Assume that the number of buses (U_t) required for a given line-haul system serving the Central Business District depends upon roundtrip time (t), capacity of bus (c), and the total number of people to be moved in a peak hour (P) in the major direction, i.e., in the morning and out in the evening.
 The formula for the number of buses required is $U_t =$
 A. Ptc   B. $\frac{tP}{c}$ C. $\frac{cP}{t}$ D. $\frac{ct}{P}$

8. The area, in blocks, that can be served by a single stop for any maximum walking distance is given by the following formula: $a = 2w^2$. In this formula, a = the area served by a stop and w = maximum walking distance.
 If people will tolerate a walk of up to three blocks, how many stops would be needed to service an area of 288 square blocks?
 A. 9   B. 16   C. 18   D. 27

Questions 9-11.

DIRECTIONS: Questions 9 through 11 are to be answered on the basis of the following information.

In 2019, a police precinct records 456 cases of car thefts, which is 22.6 percent of all grand larcenies. In 2020, there were 560 such cases, which constituted 35% of the broader category.

9. The number of crimes in the broader category in 2020 was MOST NEARLY
 A. 1,600   B. 1,700   C. 1,960   D. 2,800

10. The change from 2019 to 2020 in the number of crimes in the broader category represented MOST NEARLY a
    A. 2.5% decrease
    B. 10.1% increase
    C. 12.5% increase
    D. 20% decrease

10.____

11. In 2020, one out of every 6 of these crimes was solved. This represents MOST NEARLY what percentage of the total number of crimes in the broader category that year?
    A. 5.8
    B. 6
    C. 9.3
    D. 12

11.____

12. Assume that a maintenance shop does 5 brake jobs to every 3 front-end jobs. It does 8,000 jobs altogether in a 240-day year. In one day, one worker can do 3 front-end jobs or 4 brake jobs.
    About how many workers will be needed in the shop?
    A. 3
    B. 5
    C. 10
    D. 18

12.____

13. Assume that the price of a certain item declines by 6% one year, and then increases by 5 and 10 percent, respectively, during the next two years.
    What is the OVERALL increase in price over the three-year period?
    A. 4.2
    B. 6
    C. 8.6
    D. 10.1

13.____

14. After finding the total percent change in a price (TC) over a three-year period, as in the preceding question, one could compute the average annual percent change in the price by using the formula
    A. $(1+TC)^{1/3}$
    B. $\frac{(1+TC)}{3}$
    C. $(1+TC)^{1/3-1}$
    D. $\frac{1}{(1+TC)^{1/3}-1}$

14.____

15. 357 is 6% of
    A. 2,142
    B. 5,950
    C. 4,140
    D. 5,900

15.____

16. In 2019, a department bought n pieces of a certain supply item for a total of $x. In 2020, the department bought k percent fewer of the item but had to pay a total of g percent more for it.
    Which of the following formulas is CORRECT for determining the average price per item in 2020?
    A. $100\frac{xg}{nk}$
    B. $\frac{x(100+g)}{n(100-k)}$
    C. $\frac{x(100-g)}{n(100+k)}$
    D. $\frac{x}{n} - 100\frac{g}{k}$

16.____

17. A sample of 18 income tax returns, each with 4 personal exemptions, is taken for 2019 and 2020. The breakdown is as follows in terms of income:

Average Gross Income (in thousands)	Number of Returns	
	2019	2020
40	6	2
80	10	11
120	2	5

There is a personal deduction per exemption of $500.
There are no other expense deductions. In addition, there is an exclusion of $3,000 for incomes less than $50,000 and $2,000 for incomes from $50,000 to $99,999.99. From $100,000 upward there is no exclusion.

17.____

The average net taxable income for the samples in thousands for 2019 is MOST NEARLY
A. $67   B. $85   C. $10   D. $128

18. In the preceding question, the increase in average net taxable income for the sample (in thousands) between 2019 and 2020 is
    A. 16   B. 20   C. 24   D. 34

19. Assume that supervisor S has four subordinates—A, B, C, and D.
    The MAXIMUM number of relationships, assuming that all combinations are included, that can exist between S and his subordinates is
    A. 28   B. 15   C. 7   D. 4

20. If the workmen's compensation insurance rate for clerical workers is 93 cents per $100 of wages, the total premium paid by a city whose clerical staff earns $8,765,000 is MOST NEARLY
    A. $8,150   B. $81,515   C. $87,650   D. $93,765

21. Assume that a budget of $3,240,000,000 for the fiscal year beginning July 1, 2020 has been approved. A city sales tax is expected to provide $1,100,000,000; licenses, fees and sundry revenues ae expected to yield $121,600,000; the balance is to be raised from property taxes. A tax equalization board has appraised all property in the city at a fair value of $42,500,000,000. The council wishes to assess property at 60% of its fair value.
    The tax rate would need to be MOST NEARLY _____ per $100 of assessed value.
    A. $12.70   B. $10.65   C. $7.90   D. $4.00

22. Men's white linen handkerchiefs cost $12.90 for 3.
    The cost per dozen handkerchiefs is
    A. $77.40   B. $38.70   C. $144.80   D. $51.60

23. Assume that it is necessary to partition a room measuring 40 feet by 20 feet into eight smaller rooms of equal size.
    Allowing no room for aisles, the MINIMUM amount of partitioning that would be needed is _____ feet.
    A. 90   B. 100   C. 110   D. 140

24. Assume that two types of files have been ordered: 200 of type A and 100 of type B. When the files are delivered, the buyer discovers that 25% of each type is damaged. Of the remaining files, 20% of type A and 40% of type B are the wrong color.
    The total number of files that are the WRONG COLOR is
    A. 30   B. 40   C. 50   D. 60

5 (#3)

25. In a unit of five inspectors, one inspector makes an average of 12 inspections a day, two inspectors make an average of 10 inspections a day, and two inspectors make an average of 9 inspections a day.
If in a certain week one of the inspectors who makes an average of nine inspections a day is out of work on Monday and Tuesday because of illness and all the inspectors do no inspections for half a day on Wednesday because of a special meeting, the number of inspections this unit can be expected to make in that week is MOST NEARLY
    A. 215   B. 225   C. 230   D. 250

25.____

KEY (CORRECT ANSWERS)

1.	B		11.	A
2.	C		12.	C
3.	D		13.	C
4.	D		14.	C
5.	D		15.	B
6.	C		16.	B
7.	B		17.	A
8.	B		18.	A
9.	A		19.	B
10.	D		20.	B

21.	C
22.	D
23.	B
24.	D
25.	A

SOLUTIONS TO PROBLEMS

1. Since the number of weekly inspections ranged from 20 to 40, this implies that the average weekly number of inspections never fell below 20.

2. 591 ÷ 194 ≈ 3046, closest to 3,000 students

3. (591-268) ÷ 268 = 120%

4. Total processing cost = (268)(28) + (1,688)($21) = $42,952, closest to $40,000. [Note: Since 268 represents 13.7%, total freshman population = 268 ÷ .137 ≈ 1,956. Then, 1,956 – 268 = 1,688]

5. Let x = staff size in 2018-2019. Then, .80x = staff size in 2019-2020. Since the 2019-2020 staff produced 20% more work, this is represented by 1.20. However, to measure the productivity per staff member, the factor 1/.80 = 1.25 must also be used to equate the 2 staffs. Then, (1.20)(1.25) = 1.50. Thus, the 2019-2020 staff produced 50% more than the 2018-2019 staff.

6. The respective percent increases are ≈ 20%, 17%, 39%, 29%. The largest would be, over the previous fiscal year, for the current fiscal year 2018-2019

7. $\frac{P}{c}$ = number of buses needed per hour. If t = time (in hrs.), then U_t = tP.c

8. a = (2)(9) = 18 for 1 stop. Then, 288 ÷ 18 = 15 stops.

9. 560 ÷ .35 = 1600 grand larcenies.

10. 456 ÷ .226 = 2018; 560 ÷ .35 = 1600. Then, (1,600-2,018) ÷ 2,018 = -20% or a 20% decrease.

11. $(\frac{1}{6})(560) = 93\frac{1}{3}$. Then, $93\frac{1}{3}$ ÷ 1,600 = 5.8%

12. There are 5,000 brake jobs and 3,000 front-end jobs in one year.
5,000 ÷ 4 = 1,250 days, and 1,250 ÷ 240 ≈ 5.2. Also, 3,000 ÷ 3 = 1,000 days, and 1,000 ÷ 240 ≈ 4.2. Total number of workers needed ≈ 5.2 + 4.2 ≈ 10.

13. (.94)(1.05)(1.10) = 1.0857, which represents an overall increase by about 8.6%.

14. Average annual % change = $(1+TC)^{1/3} - 1 = (1.0857)^{1/3} - 1 ≈ 2.8\%$.

15. 357 ÷ .06 = 5,950

16. In 2020, $(h)(1-\frac{k}{100})$ pieces cost $(x)(1+\frac{g}{100})$ dollars. To calculate the cost for 1 piece (average cost), find the value of $[(x)(1+\frac{G}{100})] \div [(n)(1-\frac{K}{100})] = [(x)(100+g)/100]$. $[100/\{n(100-k)\}] = [x(100+g)]/[n(100-k)]$

7 (#3)

17.

	#	Deductions Up to 50,000		
40,000	6	2000	3000	40,000−3,000−2,000 = 35,000 × 6
80,000	10	2000	2000	80,000−2,000−2,000 = 76,000 × 10
20,000	2	2000		= 118000 × 2

35,000 × 6 = 210,000 = 210
76,000 × 10 = 760,000 = 760
118,800 × 2 = 236,000 = 236
                                1206

1206 ÷ 18 = 67

18. 2020

		Deductions			
40,000	2	2000	3000	35,000 × 2 =	70,000
80,000	11	2000	2000	76,000 × 11 =	836,000
120,000	5	2000		118,000 × 5 =	590,000
					1,496,000

1,496,000/18 = 83,111
83,111 − 67,000 = 16,111 = most nearly 16 (in thousands)

19. We are actually looking for the number of different groups of different sizes involving S. This reduces to $_4C_1 + {}_4C_2 + {}_4C_2 + {}_4C_4 = 4 + 6 + 4 + 1 = 15$. The notation $_nC_r$ means combinations of n things taken R at a time = $[(n)(n-1)(n-2)(\ldots)(n-R+1)]/[(R)(R-1)(\ldots)(1)]$. The 15 groups are: SA, SB, SC, SD, SAB, SAC, SAD, SBC, SBD, SCD, SABC, SABD, SACD, SBCD, SABCD.

20. Let x = total premiums. Then, $\frac{.93}{100} = \frac{X}{8,765,000}$ Solving, x = $81,515

21. The balance, raised from property taxes, = $3,240,000,000 − $1,100,000,000 − $121,600,000 = $2,018,400,000. Now, (.60)($42,500,000,000) = $25,500,000,000. The tax rate per $100 of assessed value = ($2,018,400,000)($100)/($25,500,000,00 = $7.90.

22. A dozen costs ($12.90)($\frac{12}{3}$) = $51.60.

23. (40(20) ÷ 8 = 100 ft.

24. Total number of wrong-color files = (200)(.75)(.20)+(100)(.75)(.40) = 60

25. Weekly number of inspections = (12×5) + (10×5) + (10×5) + (9×5) + 9×5) = 250
Subtract: 9 Monday, 9 Tuesday, 25 Wednesday
Total: 250 − 9 − 9 − 25 = 207
Closest entry is choice A.

www.ingramcontent.com/pod-product-compliance
Lightning Source LLC
Chambersburg PA
CBHW082208300426
44117CB00016B/2724